BORDER CROSSINGS

BORDER CROSSINGS

A Journey on the Trans-Siberian Railway

EMMA FICK

HARPER DESIGN

THE TRANS-SIBERIAN RAILWAY:
THE NAME ALONE EVOKES A
SENSE OF THE FANTASTICAL, THE
GRANDIOSE, THE EXPANSIVE.

EVEN BEFORE I TOOK THE JOURNEY, I
FELT A SORT OF LONGING THAT BORDERED
ON NOSTALGIA, AS THOUGH IN SOME DISTANT,
HAZY PAST I _HAD_ BEEN ON THIS TRAIN
TRIP SO EMBEDDED IN OUR COLLECTIVE
CONSCIOUSNESS. AND IT'S TRUE THAT, AS
THE LONGEST RAILWAY LINE IN THE
WORLD, THE TRANS-SIBERIAN HAS
CAPTURED THE IMAGINATIONS OF
TRAVELERS & EXPLORERS SINCE ITS
CONSTRUCTION IN THE EARLY 20TH

CENTURY, INSPIRING COUNTLESS TRAVELOGUES & RECORDS FROM THE ADVENTURERS WHO TRAVERSED SIBERIA BY TRAIN, SHARING THEIR EXPERIENCES WHETHER DELIGHTFUL, MUNDANE, OR UNPLEASANT. HERE, I THROW MY NAME IN THE HAT BECAUSE, LIKE SO MANY WHO CAME BEFORE, I WAS CHARMED & ENTRANCED BY THIS MYTHIC JOURNEY — & ULTIMATELY MOVED TO TRANSLATE THE EXPERIENCE INTO MY OWN VISUAL LANGUAGE.

OUR BACKSTORY

← THE BOOK THAT STARTED EVERYTHING

HELSINKI, FINLAND – MAY 2015

MY THEN-BOYFRIEND, NOW-HUSBAND HELVIO (he's from Brazil; we met when I was living in Serbia) AND I WERE ON A THREE-WEEK TRIP THROUGH THE BALTICS & SCANDINAVIA. IN HELSINKI ONE DAY, WE STOPPED AT A SECONDHAND SHOP, WHERE I SPENT AGES PAWING

THROUGH SCARVES. HELVIO, BORED, HOVERED NEAR THE BOOKS WAITING FOR ME TO FINISH. AFTER TWENTY MINUTES, WHEN I TOLD HIM I WAS GOING TO PAY, I FOUND HIM READING A BOOK, WHICH HE HANDED ME & ASKED ME TO BUY ALONG WITH THE SCARVES.

WHEN WE LEFT THE SHOP, HELVIO SHOWED ME THE BOOK: **TRANS-SIBERIAN HANDBOOK**. PUBLISHED IN 2007, IT HAD ALREADY TAKEN THE JOURNEY IN THE HANDS OF SEVERAL TRAVELERS, AS WE LEARNED FROM THE INSCRIPTION ON THE FIRST PAGE.

"THIS HAS BEEN MY DREAM FOR SO LONG," HELVIO TOLD ME. "MAYBE THIS BOOK IS A SIGN."

ONE YEAR LATER, WE WERE BUYING PLANE TICKETS & MAKING THE FIRST TENTATIVE ITINERARIES FOR OUR OWN TRANS-SIBERIAN EXPERIENCE. Though it was outdated & had to be augmented heavily by more up-to-date information on the web, the book remained the touchstone for our trip.

WE THUMBED ITS WELL-WORN, CURLED-CORNER PAGES WITH A KIND OF DEFERENCE, AS THOUGH THEY WERE INFUSED WITH GOOD SPIRITS OF THE ADVENTURERS GONE BEFORE US, OR AS IF THE BOOK WERE A TALISMAN WITH THE POWER TO MAKE THIS DREAM A REALITY.

EIGHTEEN MONTHS AFTER WE FOUND THE <u>TRANS-SIBERIAN HANDBOOK</u> IN A SECOND-HAND SHOP IN HELSINKI, FINLAND, WE WERE BOARDING THE TRAIN IN BEIJING, CHINA — BOOK IN HAND.

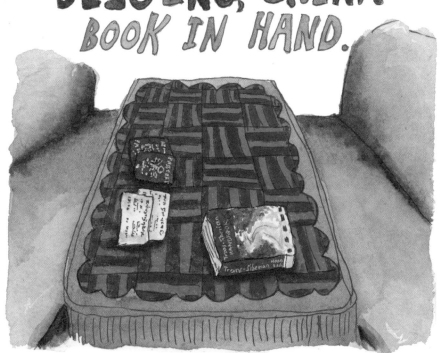

A BRIEF HISTORY OF

CONSTRUCTION ON THE TRANS-SIBERIAN RAILWAY BEGAN IN 1891 AT BOTH ENDS — MOSCOW & VLADIVOSTOK — UNDER THE RULE OF TSAR ALEXANDER III & ONE OF HIS MINISTERS, SERGEI WITTE, WHO MASTERMINDED THE PROJECT. BOTH BELIEVED THAT POLITICAL POWER RESULTED FROM ECONOMIC POWER & THAT THE RAILROAD WOULD OPEN UP SIBERIA ECONOMICALLY & INDUSTRIALLY, ALLOWING ACCESS TO ITS NATURAL RESOURCES & ENCOURAGING MORE PEOPLE TO SETTLE THROUGHOUT THE REGION. RUSSIA ALSO WANTED TO SECURE ITS EASTERN BORDER & CONTROL POSSIBLE ADVANCES FROM CHINA OR JAPAN.

ALEXANDER III ORIGINALLY MANDATED THAT THE RAILROAD BE CONSTRUCTED CHEAPLY, WHICH MEANT A NARROWER FOUNDATION, LIGHTER RAILS, & FEWER SUPPORTS ALONG THE TRACK TO KEEP THEM IN PLACE, AMONG OTHER THINGS. ULTIMATELY, THE RAILWAY COULDN'T HANDLE THE

SERGEI WITTE

DEMANDS PUT UPON IT — PARTICULARLY AFTER THE RUSSO-JAPANESE WAR IN 1904 — AND HAD TO BE RECONSTRUCTED. BUILDING THE RAILROAD ON THE CHEAP ALSO ACCOUNTS FOR MANY OF THE ROUTE'S DRAMATIC TWISTS & TURNS: THE TRACK AVOIDS

THE RAILWAY

TUNNELING THROUGH MOUNTAINS BY CIRCUMVENTING THEM COMPLETELY.

    THE GOVERNMENT SOUGHT TO RECRUIT SOLDIERS, CONVICTS, & LABORERS FROM SIBERIA & EUROPEAN RUSSIA TO BUILD THE RAILROAD. AT FIRST, MOST OF THE WORKERS WERE RUSSIAN FARMERS, PEASANTS, & PRISONERS RECEIVING REDUCED SENTENCES IN EXCHANGE FOR THEIR LABOR. LATER, SMALLER IMMIGRANT GROUPS JOINED FROM CENTRAL EUROPE & EAST ASIA.

    COMPLETED IN 1916, THE RAILROAD HAS STOOD THE TEST OF TIME. WHILE IT REPRESENTS ROMANTIC ADVENTURE FOR TOURISTS, IT'S TRULY UTILITARIAN: IT'S A POPULAR MODE OF TRAVEL FOR RUSSIANS, IF NOT A LIFELINE, & ENABLES THE TRANSPORT OF ENORMOUS AMOUNTS OF CARGO FOR BOTH FOREIGN & DOMESTIC TRADE.

TSAR ALEXANDER III

THE 3 POSSIBLE ROUTES

AN IMPRECISE, NOT-TO-SCALE MAP

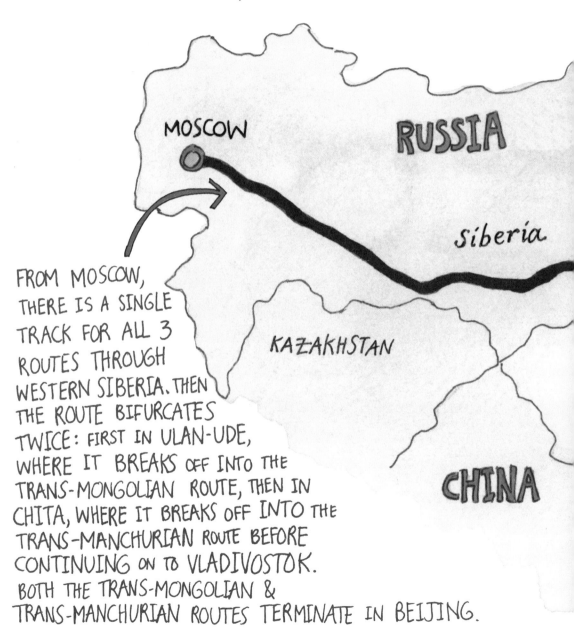

MOSCOW

RUSSIA

Siberia

KAZAKHSTAN

CHINA

FROM MOSCOW, THERE IS A SINGLE TRACK FOR ALL 3 ROUTES THROUGH WESTERN SIBERIA. THEN THE ROUTE BIFURCATES TWICE: FIRST IN ULAN-UDE, WHERE IT BREAKS OFF INTO THE TRANS-MONGOLIAN ROUTE, THEN IN CHITA, WHERE IT BREAKS OFF INTO THE TRANS-MANCHURIAN ROUTE BEFORE CONTINUING ON TO VLADIVOSTOK. BOTH THE TRANS-MONGOLIAN & TRANS-MANCHURIAN ROUTES TERMINATE IN BEIJING.

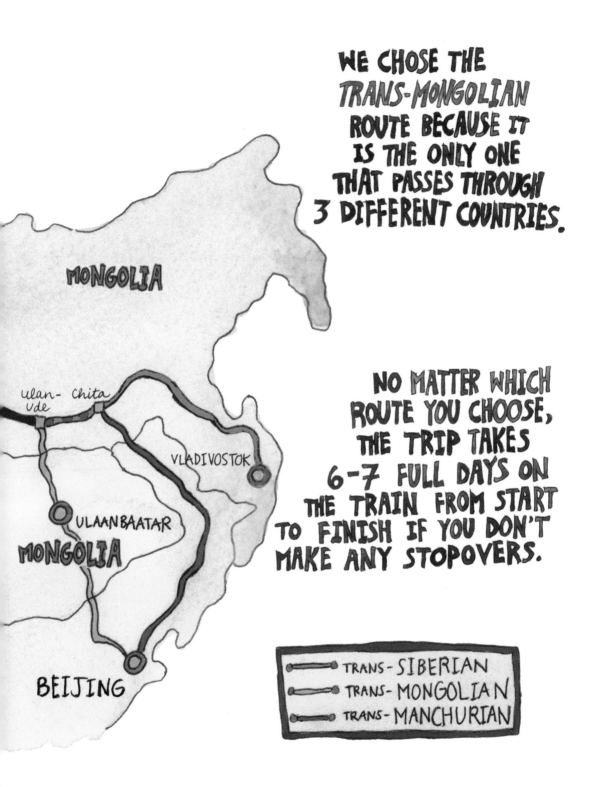

WE CHOSE THE *TRANS-MONGOLIAN* ROUTE BECAUSE IT IS THE ONLY ONE THAT PASSES THROUGH 3 DIFFERENT COUNTRIES.

NO MATTER WHICH ROUTE YOU CHOOSE, THE TRIP TAKES 6-7 FULL DAYS ON THE TRAIN FROM START TO FINISH IF YOU DON'T MAKE ANY STOPOVERS.

MONGOLIA

Ulan-Ude   Chita

VLADIVOSTOK

ULAANBAATAR

MONGOLIA

BEIJING

TRANS-SIBERIAN
TRANS-MONGOLIAN
TRANS-MANCHURIAN

OUR ITINERARY

BEIJING
MARCH 4TH

ULAANBAATAR & THE STEPPES
MARCH 5TH–16TH

IRKUTSK & LAKE BAIKAL
MAR(

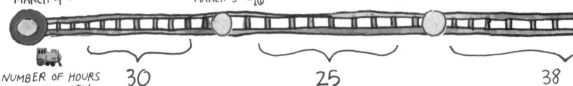

NUMBER OF HOURS ON THE TRAIN

30   25   38

IF YOU TAKE THE TRAIN FROM BEIJING TO MOSCOW WITHOUT STOPOVERS, THE TRIP TAKES ABOUT 6 FULL DAYS. WE ALLOTTED 23 DAYS TO MAKE THE JOURNEY, WITH FREQUENT DISEMBARKMENTS TO ENJOY VISITS TO TOWNS & CITIES ALONG THE WAY. THOUGH I SOMETIMES WISH WE HAD MADE MORE STOPOVERS IN DIFFERENT CITIES, THE FACT IS, THE MORE FREQUENTLY YOU DISEMBARK FROM THE TRAIN FOR OVERNIGHT STAYS, THE LESS YOU EXPERIENCE THOSE HYPNOTIC MULTI-NIGHT TRAIN RIDES. OUR REASONS FOR TAKING THE TRANS-SIBERIAN RAILWAY WERE AS MUCH ABOUT THE LONG HOURS & DAYS ON THE TRAIN ITSELF AS THEY WERE ABOUT THE PLACES WE VISITED ALONG THE ROUTE.

WE DEVIATED SIGNIFICANTLY FROM THE TRAIN ROUTE —AND SPENT THE LONGEST STRETCH OF OUR TRIP— IN MONGOLIA BECAUSE WE WANTED TO SEE THE COUNTRY'S VAST STEPPE & LEARN ABOUT THE NOMADS' WAY OF LIFE. FOR THE OTHER CITIES, STAYING A FEW DAYS IN EACH FELT LIKE PLENTY.

FOR FOREIGN TOURISTS, MAKING THE TRIP FROM WEST TO EAST IS THE MOST COMMON ROUTE, PARTLY BECAUSE MOSCOW IS EASY TO ACCESS BY PLANE, TRAIN, OR BUS AND MAKES A CONVENIENT JUMPING-OFF POINT. WE CHOSE TO GO EAST TO WEST FOR SIMILARLY LOGISTICAL REASONS: WE HAD TO GET OUR CHINESE VISAS IN HONG KONG BECAUSE HELVIO & I CARRY DIFFERENT PASSPORTS & HE WASN'T ABLE TO APPLY FOR A CHINESE VISA FROM

OMSK
MARCH 20TH-22ND

YEKATERINBURG
MARCH 22ND-24TH

NIZHNY NOVGOROD
MARCH 25TH-27TH

MOSCOW
MARCH 27TH

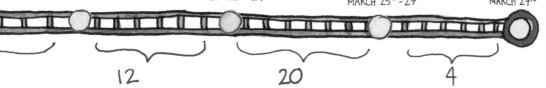

12

20

4

THE UNITED STATES, WHERE WE'D BEEN STAYING PRIOR TO OUR TRIP TO ASIA.

THE LOGISTICS OF THE TRANS-SIBERIAN RAILWAY TRIP ARE DAUNTING & THE RESEARCH REQUIRED PRIOR TO THE TRIP IS TIME CONSUMING. WHAT YOU NEED IN TERMS OF DOCUMENTS DEPENDS ON YOUR NATIONALITY. AS A US CITIZEN, I NEEDED A CHINESE VISA & A RUSSIAN VISA, BOTH OF WHICH HAVE COMPLICATED APPLICATION PROCEDURES. THE TRAIN TABLES ARE COMPLEX, THE LANGUAGES & ALPHABETS VARIOUS. THE TRAIN SCHEDULES CAN DICTATE HOW LONG YOU MAY STAY IN A PARTICULAR PLACE — OR WHETHER YOU HAVE THE TIME TO GO THERE AT ALL— BECAUSE IN SOME LOCATIONS, THE TRAIN MAY ONLY STOP ONCE OR TWICE A WEEK. SO MAKE CAREFUL NOTES, DOUBLE-CHECK EVERYTHING, AND HAVE BACKUP PLANS.

WE'RE EXPERIENCED TRAVELERS AND WE _STILL_ FOUND OURSELVES FREQUENTLY CONFUSED AND IN UNEXPECTED SITUATIONS.

MY PARTING WORDS OF ADVICE ARE: PLAN THOROUGHLY, BUT BE READY FOR ADJUSTMENT—& ENJOY THE RIDE.

PREPARING FOR THE JOURNEY

Helvio & I scheduled our trip in late February — early March. We knew we wanted to go when it was cold & snowy, but our idea of cold (I'm from Louisiana; Helvio is from Brazil) is considered warm springtime by Siberian standards. We knew to expect temperatures from about 0–40° Fahrenheit, so we bought long underwear, packable down coats, & strategic layering options in the months leading up to the trip.

Our packing issue was complicated by the fact that we were traveling for 4½ months prior to beginning our trip on the Trans-Siberian Railway. We spent almost all that time in Southeast Asia; temperatures were high, and we were in shorts & t-shirts. We had to lug around the cold-weather gear, which quickly led us to question the prudence of our plan every time we had to hoist a hulking bag onto our backs.

WE WORE THESE SMALL BACKPACKS ON OUR CHESTS. THEY CARRIED ITEMS THAT NEEDED TO BE MORE READILY AVAILABLE (BASIC TOILETRIES, A BOOK TO READ).

A TOTE BAG FOR FOOD STORES

THERMAL MUGS

PACKING CUBES ARE YOUR FRIEND. THEY KEEP THINGS ORGANIZED & SEPARATED. DIFFERENT COLORS ARE IDEAL FOR EASY IDENTIFICATION.

We did not have our exact itinerary mapped out until a few weeks before we were slated to start our trip in Beijing. Sitting under palm trees in the Philippines, hardly able to imagine snow-covered plains, we made an itinerary with corresponding dates, consulting updated online train schedules along the way. We elected to buy our tickets at each station as we went along, as opposed to buying everything in advance, because we wanted to allow maximum flexibility. This is only advisable if you go during the off-season (cold months) like we did — in the summer, tickets can sell out well ahead of time.

We got most of our information from various blogs & online resources, & we loved the wealth of knowledge on the website Seat61. We also thumbed through our trusty Trans-Siberian Handbook that we'd picked up in Finland. And, as always, we dreamed, toggling between the lore & practicalities surrounding our upcoming journey.

COMPRESSION BAGS ARE A GREAT WAY TO SAVE SPACE

NO ONE LIKES HOW MONEY BELTS LOOK OR FEEL, BUT YOU'LL HAVE TO PUT YOUR DISTASTE ASIDE: THESE ARE A _MUST_ FOR CARRYING YOUR DOCUMENTS & MONEY SAFELY. WEAR UNDER YOUR CLOTHES AT ALL TIMES ON THE TRAIN (YES, EVEN WHEN YOU'RE SLEEPING).

OUR HUGE, HULKING BACKPACKS

MARCH 4

OUR JOURNEY BEGINS!

BEIJING, CHINA

We found our way to the International Hotel to purchase our train tickets after a very confusing initial visit to the main train station. Because procuring our Chinese visas took longer than we'd anticipated in Hong Kong, combined with the fact that the Beijing-to-Ulaanbaatar train only ran twice a week, we had to limit our stay in Beijing to a single night.

WE NEEDED TO BE BACK AT THE TRAIN STATION
ONLY A FEW HOURS AFTER BUYING OUR
TICKETS AT THE INTERNATIONAL HOTEL.

OUR TICKET LOOKED LIKE THIS

When we went through the
turnstile from the station to
the platform, an attendant in
a uniform with a bright red
sash punched a hole in our
tickets, stamped them in red,
& ushered us through.

THE STAMP
& RED INK PAD

THE HOLE
PUNCH

ORIGIN: BEIJING, CHINA
DESTINATION: ULAANBAATAR,
MONGOLIA

I love this emblem featuring a folkloric winged horse

УБТЗ 525

УЛААНБААТАР ——— БЭЭЖИН
乌 兰 巴 托 ——— 北 京
ULAANBAATAR ——— BEIJING

THE SIDE OF THE MONGOLIAN TRAIN WE BOARDED

AFTER FINDING OUR COUCHETTE & PUTTING OUR BAGS DOWN, WE BUZZED AROUND THE PLATFORM TAKING IT ALL IN, TOO ANTSY WITH ANTICIPATION TO SIT STILL FOR LONG.

ON THE PLATFORM: 10:50 AM

TWO TRAIN ATTENDANTS FLANKED EACH DOOR. THEY WORE SHARP HATS & EXAMINED OUR TICKETS, LOOKING BORED (A FOIL TO OUR GIDDINESS).

Inside the train, a bright red carpet ran the length of the corridor; sliding doors gave way to each compartment.

OUR BEDS: #s 17 & 19

OUR COUCHETTE

A TRAIN COMPARTMENT WITH 4 TO 6 BEDS

LOWER BERTHS ARE HINGED & LIFT FOR LUGGAGE STORAGE.

(BERTH = FANCY WORD FOR TRAIN BED)

INSIDE, THERE ARE FOLDED BLANKETS & BEDDING.

UPPER vs LOWER BERTHS
& COMMON TRAIN COURTESY

lower

IF YOU ARE ASSIGNED THE LOWER BERTHS, KEEP THEM CLEAR OF YOUR BELONGINGS DURING THE DAY, AS THEY ARE FOR COMMUNAL SITTING. IN THE MORNING, PROMPTLY CLEAR YOUR BERTH OF ALL BEDDING SO THAT THOSE IN THE UPPER BERTHS CAN CLIMB DOWN & START THEIR DAY. IN THE EVENING, OR IF YOU WANT TO TAKE A NAP DURING THE DAY, YOU CALL THE SHOTS: WHENEVER LOWER BERTH FOLKS START TO MAKE THEIR BEDS, IT'S A SIGNAL FOR THE UPPER BERTH FOLKS TO GO UP TO THEIRS. NAPS DURING THE DAY SHOULD BE KEPT SHORT, THOUGH, AS A COMMON COURTESY. THE SMALL TABLE BY THE WINDOW TENDS TO GO TO WHOEVER IS ASSIGNED THE LOWER BERTHS, BUT IT IS KIND TO OFFER ITS USE TO YOUR COUCHETTE-MATES IF THEY ARE ABOUT TO EAT.

upper

MOST PEOPLE PREFER THE LOWER BERTH BECAUSE IT DOESN'T REQUIRE CLIMBING UP & DOWN (& BECAUSE IT AUTOMATICALLY COMES WITH THE WINDOW SEAT BY SOME UNWRITTEN RULE), BUT GETTING THE UPPER BERTH HAS ITS BENEFITS TOO! YOUR BED DOESN'T HAVE TO BE MADE & UNMADE EVERY TIME YOU WANT TO REST, & BEING TUCKED UP AGAINST THE CEILING DOES OFFER A BIT OF PRIVACY, AS IF YOU'RE IN YOUR OWN LITTLE TREEHOUSE. THE CEILING IS TOO LOW TO SIT UP COMFORTABLY, THOUGH, SO IF YOU GET THE UPPER BERTH, YOU'LL SPEND QUITE A BIT OF TIME BELOW WITH YOUR COUCHETTE-MATES.

FOR STORING SMALL ITEMS (BOOKS, WATER)
& HANGING TOWELS

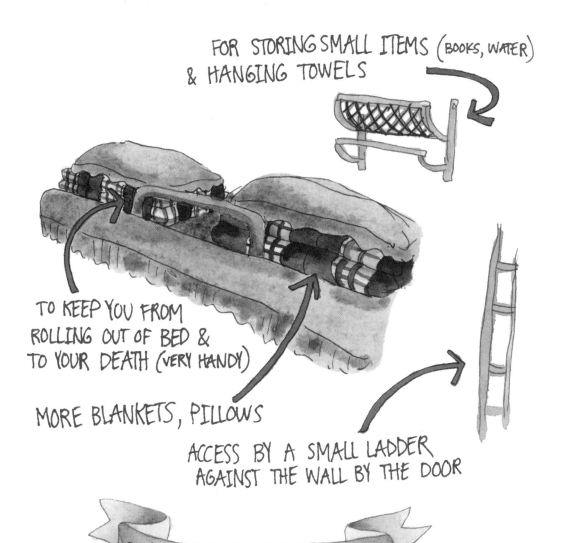

TO KEEP YOU FROM
ROLLING OUT OF BED &
TO YOUR DEATH (VERY HANDY)

MORE BLANKETS, PILLOWS

ACCESS BY A SMALL LADDER
AGAINST THE WALL BY THE DOOR

THE UPPER BERTH

NOTE: If, like us, you sometimes get the whole couchette to yourself (more common in the off-season), you have your run of the place! New passengers can get on at any time, though, so it's not a good idea to go to sleep on the bottom berth if you were assigned the top or vice versa; if you do, you might be joined by some very annoyed passengers who are wondering why there are people sleeping in their beds.

INSIDE OUR COUCHETTE, WE GOT ACQUAINTED WITH THE AMENITIES. WE FOUND A CLOTH COVERING — RED FAUX SATIN WITH SCALLOPED EDGES — & PUT IT ON THE LITTLE TABLE. THEN WE MADE OURSELVES CUPS OF TEA, & _BAM!_ INSTANT COZINESS (& we hadn't even left the station yet ✳).

✳TRAIN DEPARTED _very_ PROMPTLY AT 11:22 AM.

THE BATHROOM SITUATION

sometimes stops are long — be prepared

WC

ЗОГСОЖ БАЙХАД АЖИЛЛАХГУЙ
NOT TO USE DURING STOP TIME

don't drink water from here — only for hand-washing (I often just used hand sanitizer)

step here to flush

Western-style toilet

for showering — can't comment; never used

located right by the door. water gets the whole (tiny) bathroom wet

AS THE TRAIN LEFT THE STATION & PICKED UP SPEED, WE WANDERED DOWN THE HALL TO CHECK OUT THE BATHROOM SITUATION. THE OCCUPANTS OF EACH TRAIN CAR (UP TO 36 PEOPLE IN 2ND CLASS) SHARE 2 BATHROOMS, WHICH ARE LOCATED AT EITHER END OF THE CAR.

our saving grace

WATCH OUT; THE HOT WATER IS <u>HOT</u>! (BOILING, TO BE EXACT.)

THE HOT & COLD WATER DISPENSER — ALSO CALLED A SAMOVAR

Depending on the train, the water dispenser/samovar can either be modern (like this one, heated by electricity) or traditional (a metal urn, heated by coal).

FOOD WE BROUGHT

instant coffee

individual creamers

chocolate

peanuts, dried fruit

peanut butter

PEANU

3-in-1 spoon-knife-fork. does all three utensils' jobs poorly.

stainless steel thermal mugs with lids (mine is the yellow one)

tea bags

assorted sweet & salty crackers

noodle

instant noodles

29

We said goodbye to Beijing from our window.

The landscape changed from city to great stone mountains. Our cabin went dark & then bright like a strobe light as the train sliced through the mountains.

ICY RIVULETS BETWEEN ROCK FACES

WE SETTLED INTO THE TRAIN RHYTHM EASILY. SIPPING OUR TEA, WE LOOKED OUT THE WINDOW, WATCHING THE LANDSCAPE FLY BY, TRYING TO KEEP TRACK OF KILOMETER MARKINGS. EVERY TIME THE TRAIN STOPPED, WE THUMBED FURIOUSLY THROUGH THE TRANS-SIBERIAN HANDBOOK, TRYING TO LEARN SOMETHING ABOUT THE TOWNS WE GLIMPSED. OFTEN, THE INFORMATION WAS SPARE, SO WE ABSORBED MANY VISUAL VIGNETTES WITHOUT CONTEXT, WEAVING OUR IMAGINATIONS INTO WHATEVER INFORMATION WE HAD.

First Stop: Zhangjiakou

THREE TRAIN OPERATORS ON THE PLATFORM, TALKING & HAVING A GOOD HEARTY LAUGH. I LIKED THEIR HATS.

WHEN THE TRAIN STOPS, YOU USUALLY HAVE 10 TO 20 MINUTES TO GET OFF & STRETCH YOUR LEGS. BUT STAY CLOSE TO THE TRAIN SO YOU DON'T GET LEFT BEHIND! WE WERE ALWAYS NERVOUS ABOUT TIME, SO WE'D DISEMBARK FOR ONLY A FEW MINUTES. SOME TRAIN STOPS CAN BE LONGER, EVEN AN HOUR OR MORE, SO CHECK YOUR GUIDEBOOK TO SEE WHAT YOU CAN EXPECT.

AFTER ZHANGJIAKOU

from our window, we saw:

MANY INDUSTRIAL TOWNS:
HUMBLE BROWN-ROOF
HOUSES IN CLUSTERS BENEATH
ENORMOUS STACKS EMITTING
PLUMES OF SMOKE

SHEEPHERDERS
WITH THEIR FLOCKS

GREAT BIG METAL TOWERS,
IN VARIOUS SHAPES & SIZES,
PEPPERING THE BROWN
PLAINS

at the second stop,
JINING:

a garbage collector on the platform, wearing yellows

leaving Jining: wall with barbed wire, brown rooftops

We found ourselves sinking deeper & deeper into a train reverie punctuated by train stops. Time became fluid, & hours ran by quickly as we were lulled into some alternate universe by the rocking train & the wide landscape gliding past us through the window. The train cabins were warm; cozy & content, even in short sleeves, we remained transfixed by the view outside the window, leaving the books in our backpacks untouched.

EATING & DRINKING PROVIDED ANOTHER BREAK—IT FELT MORE APPROPRIATE TO KEEP TRACK OF PASSING TIME BY HOW MANY CUPS OF TEA WE DRANK RATHER THAN BY HOW MANY MINUTES HAD ELAPSED.

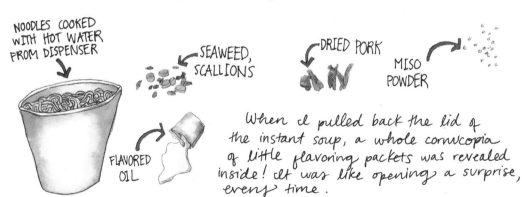

NOODLES COOKED WITH HOT WATER FROM DISPENSER

SEAWEED, SCALLIONS

DRIED PORK

MISO POWDER

FLAVORED OIL

When I pulled back the lid of the instant soup, a whole cornucopia of little flavoring packets was revealed inside! It was like opening a surprise, every time.

I couldn't wait to prepare our first meal on the train — in fact, as we progressed on the trip, Helvio joked that I always had to eat immediately after the train started moving. What can I say? Eating made me feel settled in, like I'd officially made the train compartment our home.

March 4, 7 PM

IN THE EVENING, WE WERE EXCITED TO TRY THE DINING CAR. THE FOOD SERVED IN THE DINING CARS CORRESPONDS WITH — & CHANGES ACCORDING TO — THE COUNTRY YOU'RE IN. IN THIS CASE, THOUGH WE WERE ON A MONGOLIAN TRAIN, THE DINING CAR OFFERED CHINESE MEALS. WHEN OUR TRAIN REACHED THE MONGOLIAN BORDER, THE CHINESE DINING CAR WOULD BE REMOVED; ONCE WE ENTERED MONGOLIA, A MONGOLIAN DINING CAR WOULD REPLACE THE CHINESE ONE. WE KNEW WE'D BE CROSSING THE CHINA-MONGOLIA BORDER IN THE MIDDLE OF THE NIGHT, SO THIS WAS OUR ONLY OPPORTUNITY TO TRY THE CHINESE DINING CAR OFFERINGS.

Around 7 pm, about 8 hours after we boarded the train in Beijing, we headed to the dining car, which is always at the back of the train, for dinner.

we ordered
SOUP, BEER, CHICKEN WITH GREEN PEPPER, & "CHICKEN BLOCK."

chicken & pepper

the "chicken block" was the best — had fermented bean sauce

tomato & egg soup: very little taste

a Chinese beer

34

IN THE DINING CAR

There were lights above each table; underneath the lights, the table number.

A dusty window display sat under the kitchen window, like an afterthought.

red upholstered seats with ruffles

THE CHANGING OF THE BOGIES

A FEW HOURS AFTER WE ATE DINNER WE STOPPED AT ERLIAN, A TOWN IN CHINA NEAR THE MONGOLIAN BORDER, FOR THE *BOGIE EXCHANGE*. THE BOGIE IS THE MECHANISM THAT CONNECTS THE TRAIN TO THE TRACKS, & BECAUSE THE RAILS IN CHINA ARE 3½ INCHES NARROWER THAN THE RAILS IN RUSSIA & MONGOLIA, THEY HAVE TO BE SWITCHED OUT TO ACCOMMODATE THE NEW RAIL GAUGE.

FOR A WHILE AFTER THE TRAIN STOPPED, THERE WAS STILLNESS AS THEY WENT CAR-BY-CAR TO CHANGE THE BOGIES. THEN IT WAS TIME TO CHANGE THE BOGIE ON OUR CAR, & WITH A GREAT DEAL OF SHAKING & CLANGING, OUR *ENTIRE CAR WAS LIFTED INTO THE AIR* WITH A SPECIAL MACHINE — *WHILE WE WERE STILL INSIDE!* WE PITCHED BACK & FORTH AS THEY CHANGED THE BOGIES ON OUR TRAIN CAR, & HONESTLY IT WAS PRETTY FUN!

CHANGING BOGIES IS A TIME-INTENSIVE PROCESS, TAKING 4 HOURS OR SO. DURING THIS TIME, AS AT ALL TRAIN STOPS, THE BATHROOMS WERE LOCKED, SO WE MADE SURE TO USE THE BATHROOM PRE-BOGIE EXCHANGE & LIMITED OUR LIQUID INTAKE. THE ELECTRICITY WAS ALSO SWITCHED OFF FOR THE PROCESS, SO IT GOT PROGRESSIVELY COLDER IN THE CAR.

AT 11 PM, WHILE THE BOGIE EXCHANGE WAS STILL GOING ON BUT AFTER THEY'D FINISHED WITH OUR CAR, WE DECIDED TO TURN IN. I GOT UNDER TWO THICK WOOLEN BLANKETS & SHIVERED MY WAY TO SLEEP. (ONLY IN HINDSIGHT DID WE REALIZE WHY THE TRAIN HAD BEEN SO HOT IN THE HOURS LEADING UP TO THE BOGIE EXCHANGE.)

At some point in the wee hours of the morning, we were awakened to show our passports at the Mongolian border town of Zamyn-Uud. This was a fairly fast & painless process — we groggily handed our documents over to be stamped & reviewed, then went back to sleep.

WHEN WE AWOKE IN THE MORNING, WE PULLED BACK THE CURTAINS TO TAKE IN OUR FIRST GLIMPSE OF MONGOLIA.

The sun rose over the Gobi Desert.

TRAIN LIFE MARCHED ON, HOUR BY HOUR. THE ADULTS ALL SEEMED MELLOW & CAUGHT UP IN THEIR OWN LITTLE WORLDS. WALKING DOWN THE HALLWAY WAS FASCINATING, AS YOU GOT TO GLIMPSE GROUPS OF PEOPLE — FAMILIES OR NEWLY MADE FRIENDS — EATING OR CHATTING OR DRINKING OR NAPPING OR PLAYING CARDS. THE CHILDREN WERE GOING STIR-CRAZY, THOUGH — ONE LITTLE BOY IN OUR CAR DECIDED HE'D HAD ENOUGH AFTER 26 HOURS ON THE TRAIN. HE WAS A BLUR, RUNNING UP & DOWN THE HALL & CLIMBING ON ANYTHING HE COULD FIND!

THE ATTENDANTS' QUARTERS EMITTED NEAR-CONSTANT SMELLS OF MUTTON SOUP, WHICH I GLIMPSED BUBBLING AWAY ON THEIR STOVE TOPS. I MUNCHED MY BREAKFAST BISCUITS & DREAMED OF HEARTY SOUP.

ANIMAL-SPOTTING *

cows →

← herds of shaggy camels

wild horses →

* **OUR PRIMARY TRAIN ACTIVITY,** ALONG WITH DRINKING COPIOUS AMOUNTS OF TEA.

OUR COMPARTMENT WAS OUR LITTLE COCOON, SMALL & WARM, & THE REST OF THE WORLD BEYOND OUR WINDOW— EXCEPT FOR THE FLEETING VIEW— CEASED TO EXIST.

WE'D BROUGHT A HOST OF THINGS TO OCCUPY OUR MINDS ON THE JOURNEY: PODCASTS TO LISTEN TO, BOOKS TO READ, PUZZLES TO DO, MOVIES TO WATCH. IN THE END, WE BARELY ENGAGED WITH ANY OF THEM. THE WINDOW WAS A HYPNOTIC PORTAL THAT DEMANDED OUR COMPLETE ATTENTION. THE CONTINUOUS, UNCHANGING LANDSCAPE WAS ENTRANCING, INTERRUPTED ONLY BY THE OCCASIONAL VILLAGE OR SHEPHERD WITH A FLOCK, FIELDS OF SNOW PIERCED FROM TIME TO TIME BY YELLOW GRASSES & GRAZING ANIMALS. IF I TRIED TO READ, I COULDN'T MANAGE TO GET THROUGH MORE THAN A FEW SENTENCES BEFORE RETURNING TO THE VIEW OUT THE WINDOW. THE PULL WAS MAGNETIC; THE HOURS SPED BY WITHOUT OUR NOTICING.

● ● ● ● ●

from our window, we saw:

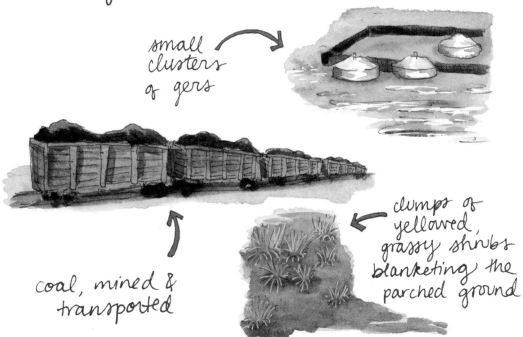

small clusters of gers

coal, mined & transported

clumps of yellowed, grassy shrubs blanketing the parched ground

WE WERE GRATEFUL FOR A STOP AT CHOIR (ЧОЙР) LONG ENOUGH TO STRETCH OUR LEGS.

ЧОЙР

The train station was beautiful. Women with grocery carts full of snacks for sale approached us from across the platform.

goods included: sodas, water, soup, instant coffee, chips, etc.

woman selling snacks on the platform

train attendants waiting diligently by each train car door (and not looking terribly thrilled about it)

WE DECIDED TO EAT IN THE DINING CAR SO WE COULD SAMPLE THE MONGOLIAN OFFERINGS. OUR PLAN WAS TO INDULGE IN ONE REAL MEAL PER DAY, MAKING THE REST OF OUR MEALS — INSTANT SOUPS, MOSTLY — WITH THE BOILING WATER PROVIDED.

AROUND NOON, WE HEADED BACK TO THE DINING CAR. THE WALK REALLY GAVE US A FEEL FOR HOW LONG THE TRAIN WAS: WE WALKED THROUGH CAR AFTER CAR FOR WHAT SEEMED LIKE AN ETERNITY. I FELT A LITTLE UNCOMFORTABLE, AS IF BY ENTERING A CAR THAT WASN'T OURS WE WERE INTRUDING IN OTHER PEOPLE'S HOMES. EACH TRAIN CAR WAS A MICROCOSM WITH ITS OWN ENERGY: SOME WERE ROWDY, SOME WERE ABSOLUTELY STILL, AND MOST WERE SOMEWHERE IN BETWEEN.

menu, slightly frayed

we could see the cooks through a little window at the back of the car

WE SELECTED OUR ENTRÉE BECAUSE IT WAS THE CHEAPEST OPTION ON THE MENU, SO IT WASN'T EXACTLY THE IDEAL FORAY INTO MONGOLIAN CUISINE. (sometimes my frugality gets the best of me.) BASED ON OUR RESEARCH, WE KNEW TO EXPECT LOTS OF LAMB AS THE PRIMARY SOURCE OF PROTEIN, AND WE'D ALSO READ ABOUT THE UBIQUITOUS MEAT-FILLED DUMPLINGS. BEYOND LAMB & DUMPLINGS, WE DIDN'T KNOW MUCH. BUT HELVIO & I ARE BOTH ADVENTUROUS EATERS, SO LEARNING MORE AS WE WENT ALONG WAS JUST FINE WITH US.

OMELET garnished with a single halved cherry tomato & some cucumber

each plate was printed with this train symbol

CARROT SALAD

AFTER LUNCH, WE TRACKED OUR PROGRESS BY MATCHING THE KILOMETER POSTS ALONG THE TRACKS TO THE KILOMETER-BY-KILOMETER GUIDE IN OUR TRANS-SIBERIAN HANDBOOK. WE COUNTED DOWN TO WHAT OUR GUIDEBOOK SAID WOULD BE IMPRESSIVE VIEWS.

WHEN WE REACHED KILOMETER 470, THE TRAIN BEGAN DRAMATICALLY SNAKING ITS WAY BACK & FORTH THROUGH ROLLING HILLS, REVEALING BREATHTAKING VIEWS OF THE ENTIRE TRAIN BEFORE & BEHIND US, THE CONVOY DWARFED BY THE SNOW-COVERED HILLS ON EITHER SIDE. WE KEPT OUR DOOR OPEN SO WE COULD DART BACK & FORTH BETWEEN THE SMALLER WINDOW IN OUR COMPARTMENT & THE WINDOW-LINED CORRIDOR, DEPENDING ON WHICH OFFERED THE BETTER VIEW. THE PANORAMA WAS SURREAL, & THE STRANGE TRAIN TIME WARP INTENSIFIED. HELVIO, MORE EASILY MOVED TO TEARS OF JOY THAN ME, BEGAN TO CRY. WE STOOD TRANSFIXED, WILLING TIME TO STAND STILL EVEN AS THE WHEELS RUMBLED BENEATH OUR FEET, REMINDING US OF OUR CONSTANT MOVEMENT.

THE UNOFFICIAL GER SETTLEMENTS SPRAWLING OUT AROUND ULAANBAATAR PROPER ARE CALLED GER _KHOROOLOL_ — THEY ARE MADE UP OF FAMILY COMPOUNDS THAT USUALLY CONSIST OF A FEW STRUCTURES, INCLUDING GERS, BUILDINGS FOR ANIMALS, & SOMETIMES HOUSES, ALL SURROUNDED BY A WOODEN FENCE TO DISTINGUISH ONE FAMILY'S LAND FROM THE NEXT. THESE KHOROOLOL ARE NOT CONNECTED TO THE CITY'S ELECTRIC OR WATER LINES.

HERE, FARTHER FROM ULAANBAATAR, THEY WERE MORE SPREAD OUT — BUT AS WE GOT CLOSER TO THE CITY, THE SETTLEMENTS BECAME DENSER & DENSER UNTIL THEY ALMOST IMPERCEPTIBLY GAVE WAY TO THE CITY ITSELF.

Reaching the outskirts of
Ulaanbaatar was our sign to start
packing our bags. We had spread
out considerably on our 30-hour
trip from Beijing! We folded our
bedding neatly, put our cold-
weather layers back on (the train
had been too hot for long underwear),
& packed our bags, ready to
disembark for our first stopover
in Mongolia's capital city.

ARRIVAL IN ULAANBAATAR

MARCH 5TH *early afternoon*

AFTER ABOUT 30 HOURS ON THE TRAIN,
WE STUMBLED OUT ONTO THE PLATFORM
IN MONGOLIA'S CAPITAL. WE WERE
IMMEDIATELY ACCOSTED BY HOPEFUL TAXI
DRIVERS. A GROUP OF THEM JOSTLED EACH
OTHER & PEERED AT THE MAP ON OUR PHONE.

THE DRIVERS DELIBERATED SO LONG & MADE SUCH A SHOW OF PEERING AT THE MAP WITH KNIT BROWS, ANIMATEDLY DISCUSSING AMONG THEMSELVES, I FEARED THE GUESTHOUSE I'D BOOKED WAS FAR OUTSIDE THE CITY. After I haggled the rate down to US $10 from $20, we got in the car... & NOT 3 MINUTES LATER ARRIVED AT THE GUESTHOUSE.

WE HAD TO LAUGH AT OURSELVES. TRAVEL IS A SERIES OF LESSONS IN HUMILITY.

WE GOT SETTLED IN OUR LOVELY FAMILY-RUN GUESTHOUSE IN CENTRAL ULAANBAATAR.

RULE #1:
IN THE HOUSE,
SLIPPERS ONLY!

IN MONGOLIA, AS IN MANY COUNTRIES AROUND THE WORLD (INCLUDING CHINA & RUSSIA), SHOES ARE REMOVED AT THE ENTRANCE OF THE HOME. WHEN YOU STEP INSIDE A DOMESTIC SPACE, YOU'LL EASILY NOTICE WHERE THE FAMILY KEEPS THEIR SHOES. THIS IS YOUR CUE: TAKE OFF YOUR SHOES & PLACE THEM WITH THE OTHERS & TAKE YOUR PICK FROM THE SLIPPERS WAITING FOR YOU, USUALLY IN A VARIETY OF SIZES.

THOUGH SOME COUNTRIES HAVE ADDITIONAL RELIGIOUS REASONS FOR REMOVING SHOES UPON ENTERING SOMEONE'S HOME, THE FOUNDATIONAL CONSIDERATION ACROSS THE BOARD IS ROOTED IN HYGIENE & CLEANLINESS. I GOT ACCUSTOMED TO TAKING OFF MY SHOES & DONNING SLIPPERS INDOORS DURING MY TWO YEARS LIVING IN SERBIA, & I SAW HOW MUCH EASIER IT WAS TO KEEP A CLEAN & COMFORTABLE HOME WITH THIS PRACTICE. IT'S ONE OF NUMEROUS CUSTOMS FROM TRAVELING & LIVING ABROAD THAT I'VE ADOPTED PERMANENTLY. THERE ARE SO MANY BEAUTIFUL (& PRACTICAL!) CUSTOMS AROUND THE WORLD THAT YOU JUST MIGHT TAKE HOME WITH YOU.

SUUTEI TSAI

OR SALTY MILK TEA

A MONGOLIAN MUST

← the _huge_ thermoses you see everywhere are usually toting it

BY ITSELF, WITH MEALS; FOR BREAKFAST, LUNCH, & DINNER; IN A CUP, IN A BOWL; ANYPLACE, ANYWHERE: SALTY MILK TEA.

SUUTEI TSAI, OR SALTY MILK TEA, IS EVERYWHERE.
YOU'LL SEE FOLKS TOTING IT ALL OVER TOWN IN HUGE THERMOSES.
THIS UNIQUE MONGOLIAN DRINK IS A SIMPLE BUT FORTIFYING
MIXTURE OF WHOLE MILK, BOILING WATER, TEA LEAVES, & SALT.
SOMETIMES ANIMAL FAT OR BUTTER IS ADDED, BUT WE FOUND THE
ADDITIONS WERE MORE COMMON OUTSIDE THE CITY: ON THE
STEPPE, THE EXTRA ENERGY IS ESSENTIAL FOR NOMAD HERDERS
TO GET THROUGH THEIR LONG DAYS OUTDOORS.

When we arrived at our guesthouse, no sooner had we donned our slippers than our hostess told us to put down our bags in our room & join her in the kitchen downstairs for some tea. The tea had already been prepared for us in its requisite huge thermos, & our hostess poured it into mugs, which she slid over to us along with some biscuits & <u>aaruul</u> (dried milk curds). She left the thermos so we could refill our cups. As our stay in Mongolia progressed, we found that each time we entered someone's home as guests, we were immediately offered suutei tsai as a welcome, along with snacks.

SUUTEI TSAI HAS AN INTERESTING SWEET-&-SAVORY FLAVOR THAT SOME VISITORS MIGHT NEED SOME GETTING USED TO, BUT WE WERE SOLD ON IT BY THE THIRD SIP. THROUGHOUT OUR STAY IN MONGOLIA, I CRAVED IT NEAR CONSTANTLY, ESPECIALLY EVERY TIME I GOT CHILLED & NEEDED A PICK-ME-UP. WE ORDERED SALTY MILK TEA WITH EVERY MEAL—IT COMPLEMENTED MUTTON DUMPLINGS PERFECTLY—& BY THE TIME WE GOT TO THE STEPPE, WE WERE SO ENAMORED OF IT THAT WE WERE THRILLED TO SEE THE ADDITION OF ANIMAL FAT, WHICH ADDED EVEN MORE FLAVOR & KEPT OUR BODIES WARM & OUR ENERGY UP THROUGH THE COLD, WIND, & SNOW.

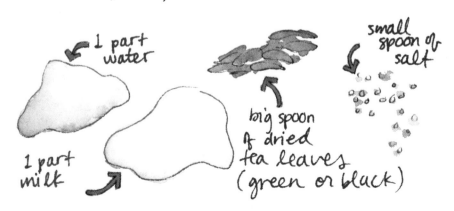

1 part water

1 part milk

big spoon of dried tea leaves (green or black)

small spoon of salt

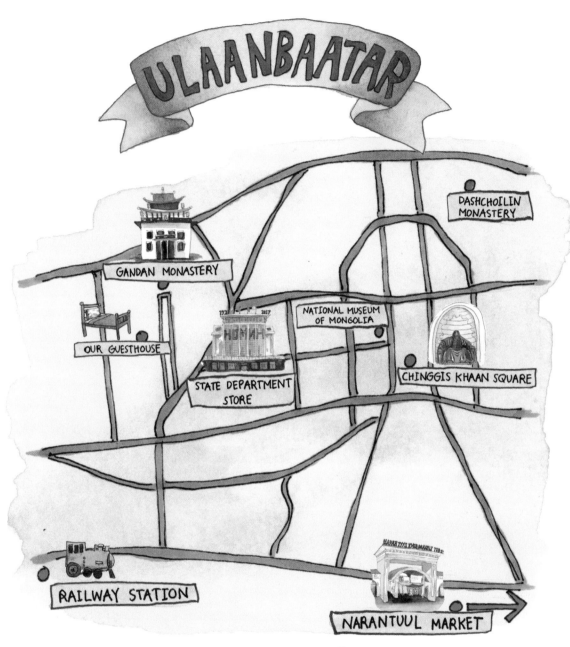

ULAANBAATAR

DASHCHOILIN MONASTERY

GANDAN MONASTERY

OUR GUESTHOUSE

STATE DEPARTMENT STORE

NATIONAL MUSEUM OF MONGOLIA

CHINGGIS KHAAN SQUARE

RAILWAY STATION

NARANTUUL MARKET

DISTANCE REFERENCE POINT: To walk from our guesthouse to Chinggis Khaan Square took about 30 minutes. Narantuul Market is quite a ways down, so going by car (hitchhiking is the norm — just flag down a car on the side of the road & agree on a price) is recommended.

OUR TWO FAVORITE SPOTS
IN THE CITY

1921 2017

STATE DEPARTMENT STORE

Established in 1921, as the roof proudly displays, this store is an institution — and a great place to buy wool & cashmere.

the central monastery, **GANDANTEGCHINLEN**, or **GANDAN** for short

GANDAN MONASTERY

GANDAN MONASTERY IS THE MOST IMPORTANT MONASTERY IN ULAANBAATAR & IS CONSIDERED THE CENTER OF MONGOLIAN BUDDHISM. IT IS AN ACTIVE RELIGIOUS SITE, WITH MORE THAN 100 LAMAS (A LAMA IS A TIBETAN BUDDHIST MONK) IN RESIDENCE TODAY. MANY MONGOLIAN VISITORS WEAR TRADITIONAL DRESS TO ENTER THE HOLY SITE, SO YOU'LL SEE A HIGHER CONCENTRATION OF FOLKS IN THEIR FINEST IN & AROUND GANDAN.

THE MONASTERY COMPLEX IS COMPRISED OF 5 TEMPLES, THE MOST IMPORTANT OF WHICH HOLDS A TOWERING 80-FOOT STATUE OF MEGJID JANRAISEG ("THE LORD WHO WATCHES IN EVERY DIRECTION"). THE ORIGINAL STATUE WAS DESTROYED BY THE SOVIETS IN THE 1930s, WHEN ALMOST ALL RELIGIOUS SITES IN MONGOLIA WERE DEMOLISHED & LAMAS WERE FORCED TO ENTER SECULAR SOCIETY & KILLED IF THEY REFUSED. IT WASN'T UNTIL THE 1990s, WHEN RUSSIAN ADVISORS WITHDREW FROM MONGOLIA & FREEDOM OF RELIGION WAS REINSTATED, THAT BUDDHISTS WERE AGAIN ALLOWED TO PRACTICE OPENLY. THE STATUE THAT STANDS AT GANDAN TODAY WAS CONSTRUCTED IN THE MID-1990s.

LION'S HEAD DOOR KNOCKER ON THE MONASTERY'S MAIN GATES

LARGE INCENSE BURNERS OUTSIDE THE TEMPLES

THE STATE DEPARTMENT STORE

WE SPENT A GOOD DEAL OF TIME IN THE STATE DEPARTMENT STORE. THE 7 FLOORS ARE DIVIDED BY THEME, MORE OR LESS: WITH JEWELRY ON THE GROUND FLOOR, FOR INSTANCE, & SOUVENIRS ON THE 6TH FLOOR. WE SPENT MOST OF OUR TIME ON THE 2ND FLOOR, PERUSING & PURCHASING CASHMERE & WOOL GARMENTS. MONGOLIA IS RENOWNED WORLDWIDE FOR ITS HIGH-QUALITY CASHMERE, & THE VERY BEST FROM NUMEROUS FACTORIES IS CONSOLIDATED & SOLD AT THE STATE DEPARTMENT STORE. IN THE END, WE STOCKED UP ON WOOL GARMENTS — ESPECIALLY YAK & CAMEL WOOL, WHICH ARE HARD TO COME BY IN MOST PLACES — BECAUSE THEY WERE MORE BUDGET FRIENDLY THAN CASHMERE WHILE STILL BEING DISTINCTLY MONGOLIAN.

THICK WOOL STRETCHY PANTS (TO THIS DAY, CALLED "MY MONGOLIA PANTS")

YAK WOOL SWEATER

SHEEP & CAMEL WOOL SOCKS

WOOL HAT →

CASHMERE GLOVES & HAT

LARGE YAK & SHEEP WOOL SCARVES →

these clothes went directly from the racks of the State Department Store & onto our bodies, where they stayed for the rest of our trip through mongolia & Russia, keeping us extremely comfortable.

A BRIEF HISTORY of CHINGGIS KHAAN 1162-1227

CHINGGIS KHAAN IS MONGOLIA'S MOST FAMOUS HISTORICAL FIGURE: A CHARISMATIC MILITARY GENIUS WHO UNIFIED THE COUNTRY'S VARIOUS NOMADIC TRIBES INTO A MASSIVE ARMY, THEN LED THAT ARMY THROUGH A SERIES OF DARING & AGGRESSIVE MILITARY OFFENSIVES THAT ULTIMATELY RESULTED IN THE WORLD'S LARGEST LAND EMPIRE. THE MONGOL EMPIRE REMAINED THE MOST POWERFUL IN THE WORLD FROM 1206 TO 1368, & CHINGGIS KHAAN REMAINS ONE OF THE GREATEST CONQUERORS THE WORLD HAS EVER KNOWN.

WITHIN MONGOLIA, CHINGGIS KHAAN IS REVERED AS A HERO & IS A SOURCE OF GREAT PRIDE. BY CONTRAST, MANY ACCOUNTS FROM OUTSIDE THE COUNTRY PAINT HIM AS A VILLAIN, LARGELY BECAUSE HIS MILITARY TACTICS INCLUDED THE MASS KILLING OF CIVILIAN POPULATIONS. FOR MONGOLS, HOWEVER, THIS IS A REDUCTIONIST ANALYSIS. CHINGGIS KHAAN'S FEATS EXTENDED WELL BEYOND HIS MILITARY PROWESS: HE ALSO ENCOURAGED LITERACY, ESTABLISHED THE COUNTRY'S FIRST CENTRAL CODE OF LAW, PROMOTED RELIGIOUS TOLERANCE, & CREATED A SINGLE NATIONAL IDENTITY FOR PREVIOUSLY DISPARATE NOMADIC TRIBES. TODAY, HE'S VIEWED UNEQUIVOCALLY AS THE FATHER OF MONGOLIA.

CHINGGIS KHAAN HAS HAD A RENAISSANCE OF SORTS RECENTLY AMONG MONGOLS — THE 1990s & EARLY 2000s SAW A DISTINCT RENEWAL OF NATIONAL INTEREST IN THE WARRIOR KING. IN 1993, SOME NOTES OF THE _TÖGRÖG_ (MONGOLIA'S CURRENCY) WERE REDESIGNED TO INCLUDE CHINGGIS KHAAN'S PORTRAIT; IN 2005, THE AIRPORT WAS RENAMED FROM _BUYANT-UKHAA_ TO _CHINGGIS KHAAN INTERNATIONAL AIRPORT_; IN 2008, A 130-FOOT-TALL STATUE OF CHINGGIS KHAAN ON HORSEBACK WAS CONSTRUCTED OUTSIDE ULAANBAATAR, MAKING IT THE LARGEST EQUESTRIAN STATUE IN THE WORLD; & IN 2013, SÜKHBAATAR SQUARE, THE CENTRAL SQUARE IN ULAANBAATAR, WAS RENAMED CHINGGIS KHAAN SQUARE (AT LEAST UNTIL 2016).

BEING REINSTATED AS A NATIONAL ICON & HERO IN MONGOLIA'S CONSCIOUSNESS IS A FITTING DESTINY FOR A MAN WHO OWED MUCH OF HIS SUCCESS TO HIS CHARISMA & HIS ABILITY TO FOSTER A CULT OF PERSONALITY.

TODAY, CHINGGIS KHAAN'S ✳ POPULARITY EXTENDS TO ALL KINDS OF COMMERCIAL GOODS AS WELL. YOU'LL FIND HIS COUNTENANCE ON CANDIES, LIQUOR BOTTLES, & SOUVENIRS. EVERYWHERE WE TURNED IN ULAANBAATAR, WE CAME FACE-TO-FACE WITH MONGOLIA'S FAMOUS CONQUEROR, WHETHER HE WAS LOOMING OVER US AS A MONUMENTAL STATUE OR LOOKING UP AT US FROM A TINY POSTAGE STAMP.

✳ A NOTE ON SPELLING:
CHINGGIS KHAAN IS THE MOST ACCURATE TRANSLITERATION FROM THE MONGOLIAN SPELLING & PRONUNCIATION, & THE VERSION WE SAW USED MOST FREQUENTLY IN MONGOLIA. GENGHIS KHAN IS THE MORE POPULAR SPELLING IN WESTERN ACCOUNTS.

CHINGGIS KHAAN EVERYWHERE:

ON POSTAGE STAMPS
postcards I sent from Mongolia took between 2 weeks & 1 year to reach their various destinations

GRACING VODKA BOTTLES

Chinggis-brand vodka is very good, & the bottle makes drinking its contents feel like a noble endeavor!

IN STATUE FORM
like in front of the government building in Chinggis Khaan Square

on the street, ulaanbaatar

the traditional coat is called a **DEEL**

deel →

high-heeled boots

A MIX OF MODERN & TRADITIONAL ON THE OLDER FOLKS: A MONGOLIAN FOLKLORIC COAT WITH A FASHIONABLE PURSE; A BIG FUR HAT WITH SLEEK LEATHER BOOTS.

FURRY!

WOOLEN!

SIMPLE!

EMBELLISHED!

THE HATS!!!!!

our first meal
IN ULAANBAATAR

After sunset, a light snow began to fall. We were cold after an afternoon of walking around Ulaanbaatar, so we decided to stop for dinner to warm up & get acquainted with the minced meat dumplings we'd read about & were excited to try. On a side street, we stopped before an eatery. From the dark, snowy road, we gazed into the restaurant's warm, illuminated interior, where a few families were eating &, to our relief—because we were tired & unfamiliar with the language—a series of large photographs posted behind the counter showed plates of food with corresponding numbers. The BUUZ we ordered were phenomenal—hearty & bursting with flavor—& we knew then & there we'd be eating very well in Mongolia.

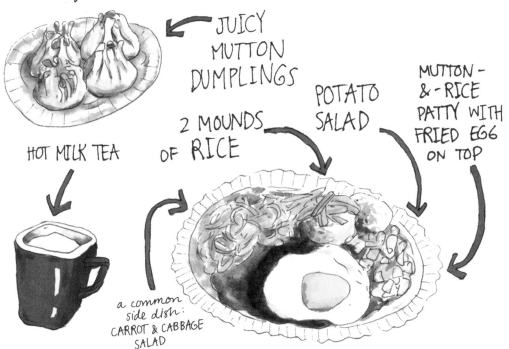

← JUICY MUTTON DUMPLINGS

2 MOUNDS OF RICE

POTATO SALAD

MUTTON-&-RICE PATTY WITH FRIED EGG ON TOP

HOT MILK TEA

a common side dish: CARROT & CABBAGE SALAD

MONGOLIAN MEAT POCKETS: AN INTRODUCTION

BUUZ, BANSH, & KHUUSHUUR

THERE ARE 3 TYPES OF MONGOLIAN MEAT POCKETS. THE DIFFERENCES BETWEEN THEM COME DOWN TO SIZE, SHAPE, & COOKING METHOD. THEY ARE ALL MADE OF THE SAME INGREDIENTS: FLOUR, WATER, ONION, GARLIC, SPICES, & MINCED MEAT, USUALLY MUTTON. HOW THEY'RE FOLDED IS A MATTER OF PERSONAL PREFERENCE, & THERE ARE MANY VARIATIONS ON THE BASIC RECIPE.

BANSH

A small dumpling. Traditionally folded into a semicircular shape. Boiled in salted water. Served alone, in soup, or in milk tea.

BUUZ

A medium-sized dumpling. Traditionally round in shape. Steamed.

KHUUSHUUR

The largest dumpling. Folded into a semicircle & deep-fried.

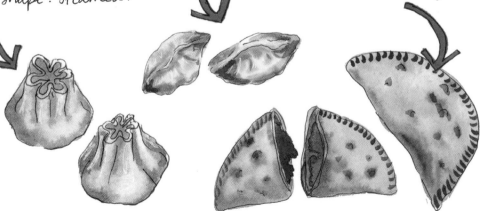

PLANNING OUR TRIP TO THE STEPPE

    BACK AT OUR GUESTHOUSE, WE CHATTED WITH OUR HOSTESS ABOUT THE ORGANIZED TRIPS SHE OFFERED. WE HAD OUR HEARTS SET ON A TRIP TO THE STEPPE TO LEARN ABOUT THE MONGOLIAN NOMADS' LIFESTYLE, BUT WE ONLY HAD A FEW DAYS TO SPEND THERE — 4 DAYS, 3 NIGHTS — BECAUSE WE PLANNED TO CATCH THE TRAIN TO ULAN-UDE ON MARCH 11. WE DECIDED TO VISIT ERDENE ZUU MONASTERY & STAY WITH NOMAD FAMILIES IN THE SURROUNDING REGION. THE GUIDE WHO NORMALLY LED TRIPS WAS NOT WORKING BECAUSE IT WAS THE OFF-SEASON, BUT THE HOSTESS HAD ARRANGED FOR A GOOD FAMILY FRIEND, ZORIGOO, WHO SHE SAID SPOKE VERY LITTLE ENGLISH, TO DRIVE US. WE REALLY WANTED TO GO, SO WE PUT THE LANGUAGE BARRIER ASIDE & AGREED.

    WE GAVE HER CASH — WHICH WAS THEN DIVIDED INTO THE APPROPRIATE AMOUNTS TO PAY EACH NOMAD FAMILY WE STAYED WITH & TO COVER THINGS LIKE FOOD & GAS — TO GIVE TO ZORIGOO. SHE ALSO FILLED A BAG WITH BREAKFAST FOOD, SNACKS, COFFEE, TOILET PAPER, & BASIC COOKWARE.

We packed a small backpack for the trip & went to sleep with visions of gers dancing in our heads.

In the morning, we met Zorigoo outside the guesthouse, then loaded our provisions & backpacks into the car trunk. It turned out that he did speak a few words of English — & those few shared words & lots of gestures enabled us to communicate just fine.

After we left the city limits of Ulaanbaatar, the landscape turned vast & bare.

WE STOPPED FOR LUNCH AT A RESTAURANT—THE ONLY STRUCTURE AS FAR AS THE EYE COULD SEE—ON THE SIDE OF THE ROAD.

rice

mutton meatballs on a bed of mashed potatoes

plenty of mutton juice

cabbage & carrot salad

salty milk tea

A MOTORBIKE RUMBLED UP OUTSIDE WHILE WE WERE EATING. TWO MEN, CHEEKS RED FROM THE COLD & THE WIND, CAME INSIDE, **ALL FABULOUS FUR SLEEVES** AND **TALL LEATHER BOOTS.**

MONGOLIA'S MOST ANCIENT SPIRITUAL PRACTICE REVOLVES AROUND WORSHIP OF THE NATURAL WORLD: SKY, TREES, RIVERS, & ANIMALS. OVER THE CENTURIES, IT EVOLVED TO FOCUS PRIMARILY ON A SINGLE GOD, _TENGRI_, WHOSE NAME TRANSLATES TO "ETERNAL BLUE HEAVEN" OR "FATHER SKY." MANY HOLY SPOTS ARE LOCATED IN ELEVATED PLACES BECAUSE THE BELIEF IS THAT BEING CLOSER TO THE SKY BRINGS A PERSON CLOSER TO TENGRI. THOUGH BUDDHISM — INTRODUCED IN THE 13TH CENTURY WHEN CHINGGHIS KHAAN CONQUERED TIBET — IS MONGOLIA'S MOST WIDELY PRACTICED RELIGION TODAY, IT IS OFTEN BLENDED WITH THE FOLK TRADITIONS OF TENGRIISM THAT PREDATED IT.

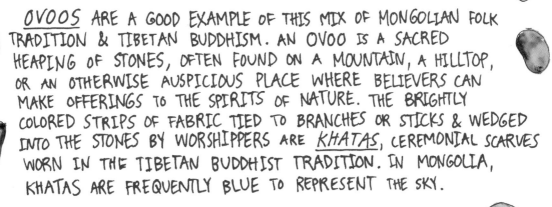

OVOOS ARE A GOOD EXAMPLE OF THIS MIX OF MONGOLIAN FOLK TRADITION & TIBETAN BUDDHISM. AN OVOO IS A SACRED HEAPING OF STONES, OFTEN FOUND ON A MOUNTAIN, A HILLTOP, OR AN OTHERWISE AUSPICIOUS PLACE WHERE BELIEVERS CAN MAKE OFFERINGS TO THE SPIRITS OF NATURE. THE BRIGHTLY COLORED STRIPS OF FABRIC TIED TO BRANCHES OR STICKS & WEDGED INTO THE STONES BY WORSHIPPERS ARE _KHATAS_, CEREMONIAL SCARVES WORN IN THE TIBETAN BUDDHIST TRADITION. IN MONGOLIA, KHATAS ARE FREQUENTLY BLUE TO REPRESENT THE SKY.

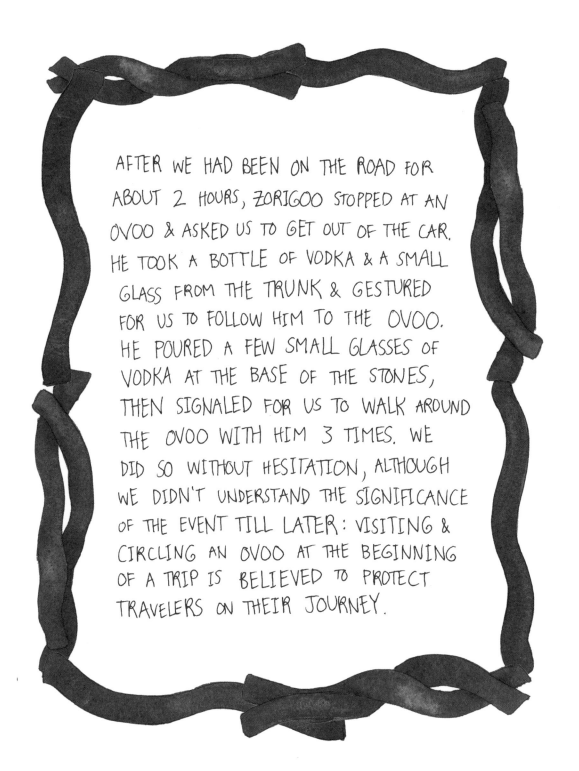

AFTER WE HAD BEEN ON THE ROAD FOR
ABOUT 2 HOURS, ZORIGOO STOPPED AT AN
OVOO & ASKED US TO GET OUT OF THE CAR.
HE TOOK A BOTTLE OF VODKA & A SMALL
GLASS FROM THE TRUNK & GESTURED
FOR US TO FOLLOW HIM TO THE OVOO.
HE POURED A FEW SMALL GLASSES OF
VODKA AT THE BASE OF THE STONES,
THEN SIGNALED FOR US TO WALK AROUND
THE OVOO WITH HIM 3 TIMES. WE
DID SO WITHOUT HESITATION, ALTHOUGH
WE DIDN'T UNDERSTAND THE SIGNIFICANCE
OF THE EVENT TILL LATER: VISITING &
CIRCLING AN OVOO AT THE BEGINNING
OF A TRIP IS BELIEVED TO PROTECT
TRAVELERS ON THEIR JOURNEY.

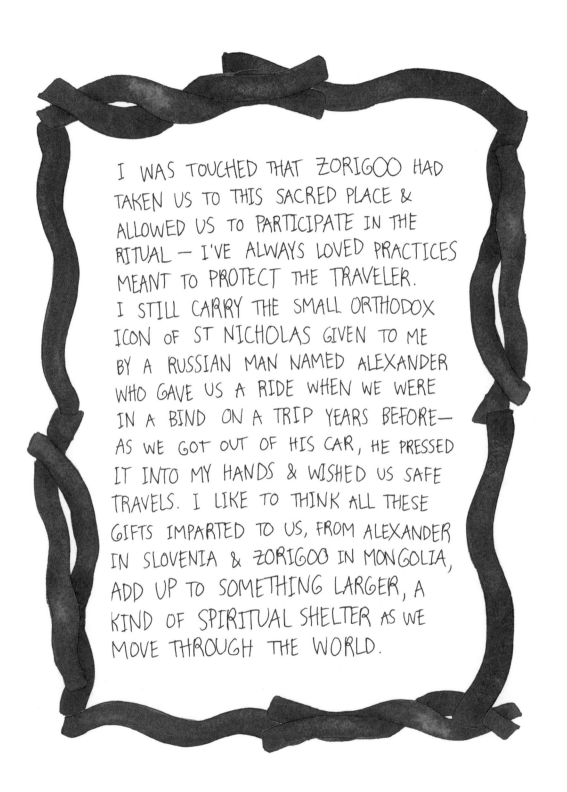

I WAS TOUCHED THAT ZORIGOO HAD
TAKEN US TO THIS SACRED PLACE &
ALLOWED US TO PARTICIPATE IN THE
RITUAL — I'VE ALWAYS LOVED PRACTICES
MEANT TO PROTECT THE TRAVELER.
I STILL CARRY THE SMALL ORTHODOX
ICON OF ST NICHOLAS GIVEN TO ME
BY A RUSSIAN MAN NAMED ALEXANDER
WHO GAVE US A RIDE WHEN WE WERE
IN A BIND ON A TRIP YEARS BEFORE—
AS WE GOT OUT OF HIS CAR, HE PRESSED
IT INTO MY HANDS & WISHED US SAFE
TRAVELS. I LIKE TO THINK ALL THESE
GIFTS IMPARTED TO US, FROM ALEXANDER
IN SLOVENIA & ZORIGOO IN MONGOLIA,
ADD UP TO SOMETHING LARGER, A
KIND OF SPIRITUAL SHELTER AS WE
MOVE THROUGH THE WORLD.

ERDENE ZUU

AFTER NEARLY A FULL DAY & ABOUT 230 MILES ON THE ROAD, WE REACHED OUR FIRST DESTINATION: ERDENE ZUU, MONGOLIA'S OLDEST BUDDHIST MONASTERY, FOUNDED AROUND 1586 & CONSTRUCTED ATOP THE ANCIENT CAPITAL CITY OF KARAKORUM. KARAKORUM WAS BUILT BY CHINGGIS KHAAN'S SON & SUCCESSOR IN 1235. THOUGH THE CITY WAS DESTROYED IN A BATTLE IN 1380, ITS RUINS PROVED USEFUL A COUPLE OF CENTURIES LATER WHEN, IN THE LATE 1500s, ALTAN KHAAN DECREED THAT ERDENE ZUU BE BUILT THERE. THE MONASTERY COMPLEX'S 4 PERIMETER WALLS— EACH OF WHICH MEASURES ABOUT 1,300 FEET LONG, OR MORE THAN 3½ FOOTBALL FIELDS — WERE CONSTRUCTED USING RUBBLE FROM KARAKORUM.

AT ITS PEAK, THE ERDENE ZUU MONASTERY COMPLEX HAD AN ESTIMATED 100 TEMPLES & MORE THAN 1,000 LAMAS. FROM 1939 TO 1990, DURING THE COMMUNIST REGIME'S RELIGIOUS PURGES, MOST OF ERDENE ZUU'S TEMPLES WERE DESTROYED. BUT ERDENE ZUU IS ONE OF ONLY A HANDFUL OF BUDDHIST MONASTERIES IN MONGOLIA THAT ESCAPED TOTAL DESTRUCTION UNDER COMMUNISM, LIKELY BECAUSE IT WAS USED AS A SYMBOL OF RELIGIOUS TOLERANCE THAT THE REGIME WOULD SHOW VISITING DIGNITARIES FROM DEMOCRATIC NATIONS.

ERDENE ZUU BECAME AN ACTIVE MONASTERY AGAIN IN 1997, THOUGH THE MAIN TEMPLE COMPLEX STILL SERVES AS A MUSEUM FOR VISITORS.

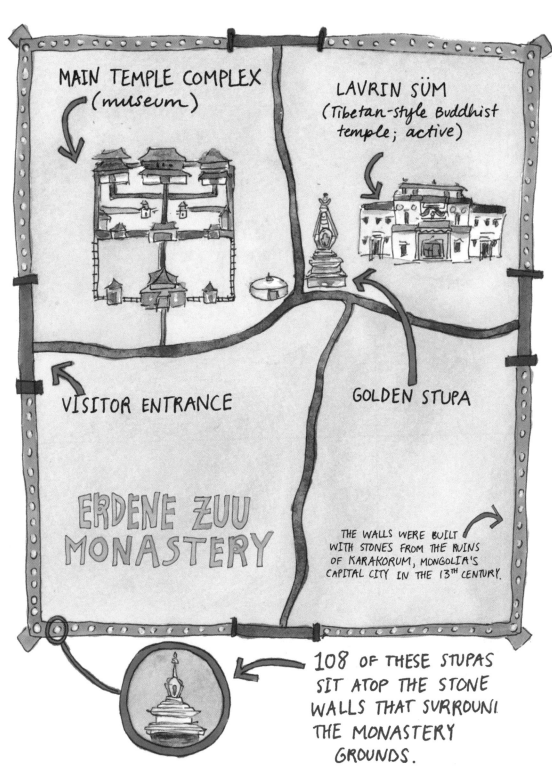

MAIN TEMPLE COMPLEX
(museum)

LAVRIN SÜM
(Tibetan-style Buddhist
temple; active)

VISITOR ENTRANCE

GOLDEN STUPA

ERDENE ZUU
MONASTERY

THE WALLS WERE BUILT
WITH STONES FROM THE RUINS
OF KARAKORUM, MONGOLIA'S
CAPITAL CITY IN THE 13TH CENTURY.

108 OF THESE STUPAS
SIT ATOP THE STONE
WALLS THAT SURROUND
THE MONASTERY
GROUNDS.

OFFERINGS ARE LEFT OUTSIDE THE GOLDEN STUPA, ONE OF THE FEW STRUCTURES AT ERDENE ZUU TO SURVIVE THE RELIGIOUS PURGES DURING COMMUNISM.

various breads & cakes, candies, tissues, money, rocks, water, sugar cubes, etc.

BUDDHIST STUPAS HOLD HOLY RELICS & ARE PLACES FOR MEDITATION & REFLECTION. THE OFFERINGS WE OBSERVED WERE YET ANOTHER EXAMPLE OF MONGOLIAN FOLK BELIEFS BLENDING WITH TIBETAN BUDDHISM: GIFTS OF DAIRY, OR "WHITE FOODS," AS THEY'RE CALLED IN MONGOLIA, CARRIED OVER FROM THE ANCIENT FOLK PRACTICE OF OFFERING MILK PRODUCTS TO THE SPIRITS OF THE NATURAL WORLD.

THE GOLDEN STUPA

LAVRIN SÜM

LAVRIN SÜM IS AN ACTIVE TIBETAN TEMPLE & MONASTERY — & WAS THE HIGHLIGHT OF OUR VISIT TO ERDENE ZUU. WE FOLLOWED THE FLOW OF TRAFFIC PAST THE PRAYER WHEELS, AROUND THE GOLDEN STUPA, & TOWARD LAVRIN SÜM. WE HEARD CHANTING AS WE APPROACHED, & WHEN WE WALKED THROUGH THE DOOR ON THE LEFT SIDE OF THE TEMPLE, WE FOUND OURSELVES IN A SMALL DARK ROOM FRAGRANT WITH INCENSE & FULL OF CHANTING MONKS & MONGOLIAN WORSHIPPERS, ABOUT 15 PEOPLE TOTAL. WE STOOD QUIETLY FOR A LITTLE WHILE, THEN HEADED TO THE RIGHT SIDE OF THE TEMPLE.

inside Lavrin süm

BEHIND THE TEMPLE'S RIGHT-HAND DOOR, WE FOUND A
BRIGHTLY LIT ROOM PAINTED FLOOR-TO-CEILING WITH TRADITIONAL
TIBETAN DECORATIVE MOTIFS. THERE WERE CUBBIES FOR MONKS'
ROBES & THE WALLS WERE COVERED IN FRAMED <u>THANGKAS</u>, OR
BUDDHIST SCROLL PAINTINGS.

thangkas, Buddhist
scroll paintings, cover
the walls

hats
& cubbies
holding
the lamas'
robes

THE BRIGHTLY PAINTED INTERIOR IS TYPICAL OF TIBETAN DECORATIVE ARTS.

the beautifully painted wood-paneled ceiling

painted pillars

a heavy embroidered tapestry hangs at one entrance

TIBETAN PRAYER WHEELS ARE A COMMON
SIGHT AROUND MONGOLIA'S BUDDHIST TEMPLES.
THE WHEELS, OFTEN METAL, HOUSE TIGHTLY
WOUND PAPER SCROLLS INSCRIBED WITH MANTRAS.
WHEN VISITORS SPIN THE WHEELS, THOSE
MANTRAS ARE RELEASED OUT INTO THE WORLD.
THE WHEELS ARE ALWAYS SPUN CLOCKWISE.

a family spinning
the prayer wheels as
they approach
Lavrin Süm temple

THE MOST IMPORTANT ARTICLE OF TRADITIONAL MONGOLIAN CLOTHING, WORN BY MEN & WOMEN ALIKE, IS CALLED A **DEEL**. IT'S A TUNIC-LIKE GARMENT WITH A ROUNDED COLLAR THAT BUTTONS AT THE RIGHT SHOULDER. IT REACHES BELOW THE KNEES & HAS EXTREMELY LONG SLEEVES THAT COVER THE WEARER'S HANDS TO PROTECT THEM, MUCH AS GLOVES WOULD. IN THE SUMMER, NOMADS WEAR DEELS OF COTTON OR SILK; IN THE WINTER, THEY WEAR THICK COTTON DEELS LINED WITH SHEEPSKIN. A SASH OF CONTRASTING COLOR IS TIED AT THE WAIST.

IN NOMAD CULTURE DEELS ARE WORN DAILY: SOME ARE DONNED FOR EVERYDAY WORK & ALLOWED TO GET DIRTY & WORN, WHILE OTHERS, MADE OF FINER FABRICS & WITH MORE ELABORATE DECORATIONS, ARE SAVED FOR FORMAL EVENTS. IN MONGOLIAN CITIES, WESTERN-STYLE CLOTHING IS MORE COMMON, BUT EVERYONE HAS A SPECIAL DEEL AT HOME THAT THEY CAN WEAR FOR NOTEWORTHY OCCASIONS.

Mongolian dress has beauty & presence. The folkloric decorations, the vibrancy of the fabrics, the furs peeking out — it is an absolute symphony of colors, textures, & forms that brightens everything around. I felt terribly drab in my black & gray clothes.

in the parking lot, a single
motorbike, draped in a
fur pelt

MARCH 6, evening

WE SPENT THE NIGHT IN A GER ENCAMPMENT JUST A FEW MINUTES' DRIVE FROM ERDENE ZUU. WE WOULD HAVE PREFERRED TO STAY WITH A NOMAD FAMILY, BUT THERE WASN'T ENOUGH TIME TO MAKE THE LONG DRIVE FROM ULAANBAATAR, VISIT THE MONASTERY, & MAKE IT OUT TO A NOMAD FAMILY'S GER ALL IN ONE DAY.

YOU RESERVE A GER AT AN ENCAMPMENT JUST AS YOU RESERVE A ROOM AT A HOTEL. OUR GER HAD 5 TWIN BEDS LINING THE PERIMETER — HELVIO & I CHOSE TWO OFF TO ONE SIDE, & ZORIGOO PICKED ONE ON THE OTHER — A STOVE IN THE MIDDLE, & NOT MUCH ELSE. THE BATHROOM, A SMALL WOODEN STRUCTURE BUILT AROUND A HOLE IN THE GROUND, WAS LOCATED OUTSIDE THE CLUSTER OF GERS & SHARED BY THE WHOLE CAMP.

BECAUSE WE WERE THERE IN THE OFF-SEASON, WE WERE THE ONLY GUESTS AT THE CAMP THAT NIGHT.

Our stay was a good basic introduction to the ger, but it was sterile, almost like a museum. The space lacked the lived-in spirit that we'd experience in the following days when we were the guests of nomad families.

The ger camp owner loaded our stove with dried cow dung — which burns with no smell at all — & the space was toasty in no time. We read about gers in our guidebook, looking around us to connect the words on the page to the structure over our heads.

GERS

GERS — TRADITIONAL MONGOLIAN DWELLINGS — ARE INGENIOUS STRUCTURES. THEY ARE PORTABLE, LIGHTWEIGHT, EASY TO PUT UP & TAKE DOWN, YET INCREDIBLY SECURE & IMPENETRABLE TO THE ELEMENTS. THE COMBINATION OF PORTABILITY & STRENGTH IS ESSENTIAL BECAUSE NOMAD FAMILIES MOVE THEIR HOME BASE WITH THE CHANGE OF THE SEASONS. SEASONAL MOVES ENSURE THE NOMADS' HERDS HAVE FRESH PASTURES ON WHICH TO GRAZE. BECAUSE EACH FAMILY RETURNS TO THE SAME 4 HOME BASES EVERY YEAR, THEY ARE SURE TO FIND UNTOUCHED PASTURES. THEY ALSO DON'T HAVE TO WORRY ABOUT ANOTHER FAMILY SETTING UP RESIDENCE IN THEIR SPOT: THE NETWORK OF MOVING NOMAD FAMILIES IS AN ELABORATE & COOPERATIVE DANCE.

Most families can put up their ger from start to finish in a few hours. First, collapsible wooden lattice panels (KHANA) are extended & tied to one another with thin ropes to form the outer walls, then a wooden door is put in place to complete the circle. The next step is to erect 2 thick wooden pillars (BAGANA) that stand floor-to-ceiling at the center of the ger to anchor the roof's central ring (TOONO). Then, thin wooden poles (UNI) are affixed to the TOONO, radiating outward to connect to the KHANA, thus completing the ger's structural framework. Some families may put down wood flooring too, but it is more common to layer thick carpets on the ground.

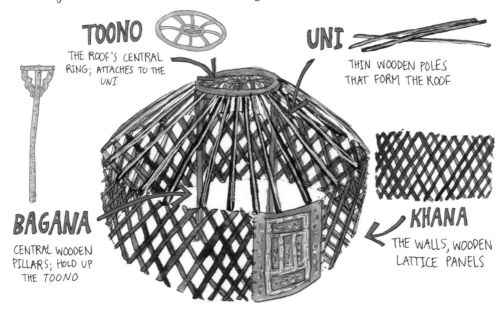

TOONO
THE ROOF'S CENTRAL RING; ATTACHES TO THE UNI

UNI
THIN WOODEN POLES THAT FORM THE ROOF

BAGANA
CENTRAL WOODEN PILLARS; HOLD UP THE TOONO

KHANA
THE WALLS, WOODEN LATTICE PANELS

After the wooden elements are in place, the frame is covered completely with rolls of felt made from sheep's wool — all except for the TOONO, which remains partly open to allow fresh air & light in & to accommodate the pipe that funnels out smoke from the powerful stove beneath it. Finally, waterproof canvas is put atop the felt layers & tied in place by wrapping horsehair rope around the whole ger.

THE GER INTERIOR

THE INTERIOR SETUP OF A GER IS FAIRLY CONSISTENT. THE STOVE SITS BETWEEN THE *BAGANA* (THE TWO CENTRAL UPRIGHT PILLARS).

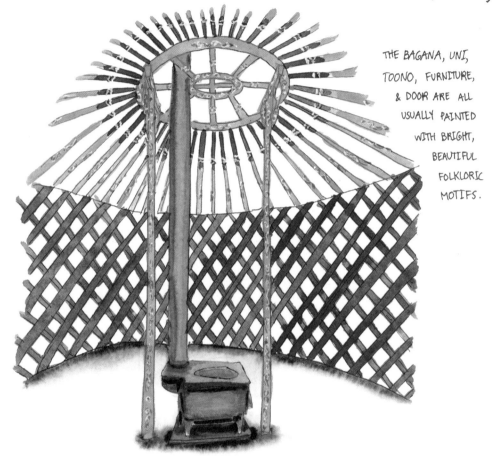

THE BAGANA, UNI, TOONO, FURNITURE, & DOOR ARE ALL USUALLY PAINTED WITH BRIGHT, BEAUTIFUL FOLKLORIC MOTIFS.

BEHIND THE STOVE, TOWARD THE BACK WALL, ARE A TABLE & A FEW STOOLS. ALL OTHER FURNITURE — INCLUDING BEDS, CHESTS, & CUPBOARDS — IS PUSHED AGAINST THE PERIMETER OF THE GER SO THE CENTER SPACE IS KEPT CLEAR. BEDDING IS FOLDED NEATLY FIRST THING IN THE MORNING, AS THE BEDS SERVE AS SEATING DURING THE DAY. THE WALLS ARE OVERLAID WITH DECORATIVE SHEETS TO COVER THE *KHANA* (LATTICE PANELS THAT FORM THE WALLS).

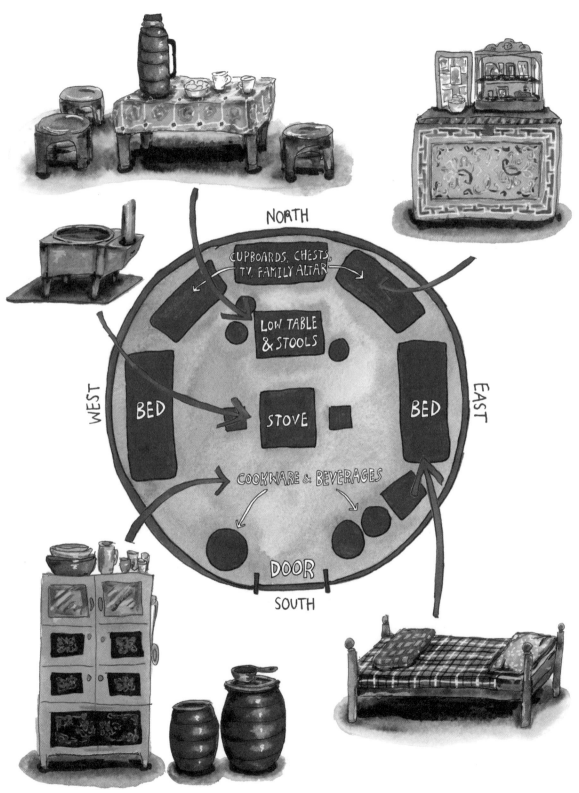

NORTH

CUPBOARDS, CHESTS, TV, FAMILY ALTAR

LOW TABLE & STOOLS

WEST

BED

STOVE

EAST

BED

COOKWARE & BEVERAGES

DOOR

SOUTH

93

THE NOMAD'S ALTAR

At the back of the ger, across from the door, nomad families have an "altar" where they display family photographs, precious objects, and, if they're religious, Buddhas, incense, & the like. The ones I saw utilized this kind of triptych of decorated wooden panels.

THE GER DOOR
DECORATED WITH *ENDLESS KNOTS*

Most doors are decorated with some variation of THE ENDLESS KNOT, one of the 8 auspicious symbols in Buddhism, which represents the infinite wisdom & compassion of Buddha.

DRIED COW DUNG IS USED AS FUEL

& frequently shoveled into the stove. I hadn't registered that in a landscape so devoid of trees, the nomads had to get their fire fuel elsewhere.

To me, the ger looked small from the outside – probably because I was comparing it to the vast landscape around it – but when I crossed the threshold, I felt as if I were passing through a magic portal behind which space ballooned improbably. The interior revealed itself to be spacious & open – even with 10 people inside – yet cozy. The interior world of Mongolian nomads is opulent & spacious, an apt complement to the visual bounty of their natural surroundings: passing through the ger's threshold, whether from inside out or from outside in, I marveled at the vastly different but equally remarkable worlds that awaited me on either side.

THE GER ENCAMPMENT OWNER BROUGHT US A DINNER
OF BUUZ & CABBAGE & CARROT SALAD. AFTER WE ATE,
WE READ A BIT MORE, THEN GOT IN OUR BEDS. WE TRIED
TO GO TO SLEEP, BUT IT WAS STIFLING HOT — OUR
FIRST LESSON IN THE INCREDIBLE EFFICACY OF THE GER'S
FELT INSULATION — & WE HAD TO OPEN THE DOOR A CRACK.

our enormous
milk tea
thermos

ZORIGOO'S
HELVIO'S

salty
milk tea
(SUUTEI
TSAI)

mutton
dumplings
(BUUZ)

MINE

cabbage
& carrot
salad

MARCH 7, 7 AM

Overnight, the fire dwindled & went out; we awoke quite cold. Zorigoo lit another fire & we were toasty in no time. When we swung open the ger door, we discovered a thick snow had fallen overnight. Everything was a luminous white.

After coffee & scrambled eggs — which Helvio made on the stove with provisions our Ulaanbaatar hostess had given us — we packed up & prepared for another day on the road. The day's itinerary: visit some archaeological sites around Karakorum, then stay with a nomad family.

The snow was so thick that the car got stuck on the way out from the encampment. Zorigoo had me take the driver's seat as he & Helvio pushed the car from behind until it found some traction. We made it to the main road with no further mishaps.

ZORIGOO PULLED OFF THE ROAD, PARKED THE CAR, GOT OUT,
AND THEN MOTIONED FOR US TO FOLLOW HIM. HE SET OFF—
WE FOLLOWED, UNSURE WHERE WE WERE HEADED. GIVEN
THE FRESH SNOWFALL, IT WAS AN ARDUOUS WALK. WE
SLOGGED THROUGH THE SNOW — SOMETIMES UP TO OUR KNEES—
BUT IT WAS WORTH THE REWARD: VIEWS OF WILD HORSES
IN AN UNBROKEN SEA OF WHITE.

A FEW MINUTES' WALK PAST THE WILD HORSES, WE ARRIVED AT OUR DESTINATION: TWO ARCHAEOLOGICALLY & SPIRITUALLY SIGNIFICANT STONES.

The stones were not that big — they only reached to a bit above my knees — & each stone was enclosed in an iron fence.
Visitors had tied dozens of blue KHATAS (Tibetan shawls) around the fence.

TURTLE STONE

THIS IS 1 OF THE 4 TURTLE STATUES THAT MARKED THE 4 CORNERS OF THE ANCIENT CAPITAL CITY OF KARAKORUM. TODAY, ONLY 2 OF THE 4 REMAIN. TURTLES SYMBOLIZE ETERNITY & PROTECTION.

THE PHALLIC STONE/PENIS STONE

THIS STATUE WAS MEANT TO REMIND YOUNG MONKS IN KARAKORUM TO REMAIN CELIBATE. TODAY, WOMEN VISIT & SIT ON IT TO PROMOTE FERTILITY. ZORIGOO WOULDN'T LET US LEAVE UNTIL I SAT ON IT, SO I GAVE IT A WHIRL. I CAN'T SPEAK TO ITS EFFICACY AS FAR AS FERTILITY GOES — MY MAIN TAKEAWAY WAS THAT THE STONE WAS VERY COLD!

TSUIVAN
CLEAR-BROTH STEW
WITH THICK-CUT
NOODLES & STRIPS
OF MUTTON

SALTY
MILK
TEA

KHUUSHUUR

AT LUNCH, ZORIGOO COMMUNICATED THAT WE WOULD SPEND THE REMAINDER OF THE DAY FINDING A NOMAD FAMILY TO STAY WITH. THERE WAS NO PLAN—WE WOULD SIMPLY SEE WHERE WE ENDED UP.

● ● ● ● ○

ZORIGOO DROVE A FEW HOURS ON ROADS THAT ALL LOOKED ALIKE AS FAR AS WE COULD TELL—THERE WERE NO LANDMARKS TO SPEAK OF. THEN, SEEMINGLY AT RANDOM, WE PULLED OFF ON A SMALLER ROAD & APPROACHED A NOMAD FAMILY'S COMPOUND, MADE UP OF 2 GERS & HUNDREDS OF ANIMALS.

A TEENAGE GIRL CAME OUT WHEN OUR CAR PULLED UP, & ZORIGOO ASKED IF WE COULD STAY FOR THE NIGHT. HE DIDN'T SEEM TO EVEN ENTERTAIN THE POSSIBILITY THAT THE ANSWER TO OUR REQUEST WOULD BE NO, AS ACCEPTING GUESTS IS A CENTRAL & ANCIENT PART OF NOMAD CULTURE.

THE GIRL WENT INSIDE TO CALL HER FATHER, WHO WAS OUT IN THE STEPPE WITH HIS HERDS, TO ASK HIS PERMISSION (NOWADAYS SOLAR PANELS ALLOW NOMAD FAMILIES TO CHARGE CELL PHONES & OTHER ELECTRONIC DEVICES). HE SAID YES, & THE GIRL APPEARED AGAIN WITH HER MOTHER TO WELCOME US INSIDE.

BETWEEN NOMADS NO MONEY IS EXCHANGED FOR LODGING—ANY FAMILY WILL WELCOME ANOTHER INSIDE WITHOUT QUESTION. IN OUR CASE, MONEY WAS NOT DISCUSSED — PERHAPS IT WAS NOT EVEN EXPECTED — WHEN WE WERE INVITED IN. HOWEVER, IT IS NORMAL (& IN MY OPINION, MORAL) FOR TOURISTS TO PAY THE FAMILIES THEY STAY WITH. WE SAW ZORIGOO PRESS MONEY INTO THE FATHER'S HAND WHEN WE DEPARTED THE NEXT DAY, BUT HELVIO & I HAD NO KNOWLEDGE OF THE AMOUNT OR THE PROTOCOL & WERE GRATEFUL TO ZORIGOO FOR HANDLING THE DETAILS.

basketball hoop on small slab of cement

ger for parents & 3 of the 4 kids: teenage girl, 10-year-old boy, toddler girl

permanent structure for animals (goats & sheep)

ger of eldest son (around 20) & his brand-new wife

solar panels power TV & indoor freezer

THE BOY
youngest son

THE FATHER

THE MOTHER
& her toddler
daughter — a little
tyrant!

THE ELDEST SON

THE ELDEST
SON'S WIFE

THE GIRL
*eldest
daughter*

The Nomad Family

THE TABLE OF OFFERINGS

AIRAG

SLIGHTLY FIZZY RED FRUIT DRINK

SUUTEI TSAI (SALTY MILK TEA)

A BOWL OF HARD CANDIES

OUR TWO MILK TEAS, SERVED IN BOWLS

LEFTOVER UL BOOV WITH AARUUL (DRIED MILK CURDS)

the lightly fizzy red fruit drink was ladled from this large blue plastic drum along the wall.

UL BOOV IS MADE OF LAYERS OF THESE FRIED CAKES & TOPPED WITH AARUUL (DRIED MILK CURDS), SUGAR CUBES, & HARD CANDIES

it is traditionally made for the Lunar New Year

fried cakes that look like the bottom of a shoe, or footprints in snow

THIS BEAUTIFUL SILVER SET IS TAKEN OUT FOR SPECIAL OCCASIONS

AIRAG
fermented mare's milk. Tangy, a little bit fizzy. ONLY 2-3% ALCOHOL CONTENT.

MONGOL ARKHI (homemade). ARKHI is made from fermented milk/yogurt. 15-20% ALCOHOL CONTENT.

MARCH 7, afternoon

After we ate & drank & exchanged pleasantries, we headed outside to explore. The boy was very helpful & engaged: he hopped on a motorbike to herd animals toward us & gave us a tour of the ger compound. He also showed us how the family kept its meat, the main food source through winter, on a raised platform outside. They used the elements to their advantage: the wind & cold weather dry & preserve the meat naturally.

Whole cows are dried in bags over the winter — this meat will provide sustenance during the summer, though nomads eat very little meat at that time of year.

THE YOUNG BOY CLAMBERED UP & PULLED OFF A PIECE OF MEAT FOR US TO TRY — TASTY!

• • • • •

to pass the time, we:

DRANK LOTS OF SALTY MILK TEA

SHOT SOME BASKETS IN THE NET-LESS HOOP WITH THE BOY

PLAYED CHESS (I LOST _BADLY_) & A TRADITIONAL GAME WITH SHEEP ANKLEBONES

SHAGAI : SHEEP ANKLEBONES, USED FOR GAME PLAYING & FORTUNE TELLING

each side of the bone has a distinct shape & represents a herd animal:

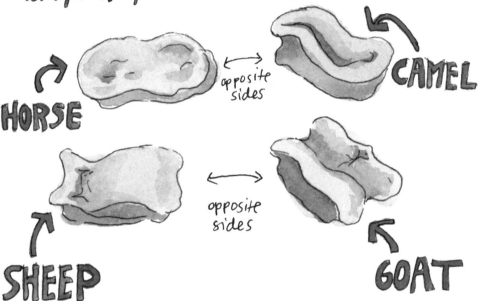

HORSE

opposite sides

CAMEL

SHEEP

opposite sides

GOAT

THE BOY TAUGHT US THE SIMPLEST GAME, "HORSE RACING," USUALLY PLAYED BY ONLY THE VERY YOUNGEST CHILDREN, PROBABLY BECAUSE IT WAS THE ONLY GAME POSSIBLE TO EXPLAIN WITHOUT WORDS. (ANIMAL DESIGNATIONS WERE COMMUNICATED WITH NOISES & DRAWINGS ~ *EASY!*)

① PICK YOUR PLAYING PIECE: *an ankle-bone with some distinguishing quality* (SOME ARE DYED COLORS FOR THIS PURPOSE). THIS IS YOUR HORSE.

② MAKE A LINE of SHAGAI.
This is your RACETRACK.

(CONTINUED FOR AT LEAST 12 PIECES)

③ LINE UP THE PLAYERS' HORSES AT THE STARTING POINT.

④ THROW A SET OF 4 BONES LIKE DICE.
THE NUMBER THAT LAND ON THE *HORSE* SIDE OF THE PIECE EQUALS THE NUMBER OF SPACES YOU CAN MOVE FORWARD.

⑤ WHOEVER REACHES THE END OF THE TRACK FIRST *WINS!*

WE MET THE FAMILY'S MANY ANIMALS.

MONGOLIAN HERDS ARE MADE UP OF <u>TAVAN HOSHUU MAL</u>, OR "THE FIVE SNOUTS" : COWS, CAMELS, GOATS, HORSES, & SHEEP. IT'S NOT UNUSUAL FOR A NOMAD FAMILY TO HAVE UPWARD OF 1,000 ANIMALS. NOMADS' RELIANCE ON THEIR FLOCKS CANNOT BE OVERSTATED. THEY RELY ON THEIR ANIMALS FOR FOOD, CLOTHING, TRANSPORTATION, & MORE. NOMADS MAKE FELT FROM WOOL TO INSULATE THEIR GERS, & MAKE ROPE FROM HORSES' HAIR. WHEN IT COMES TO FOOD, MEAT FROM SHEEP IS THE MOST COMMON, & MEAT FROM GOATS, CATTLE, & YAK IS CONSUMED ONLY OCCASIONALLY.

the 5 domesticated animals (& food sources) in Mongolia

GOAT

SHEEP

HORSE

CAMEL

COW/YAK

THE BACTRIAN CAMEL, ALSO KNOWN AS THE MONGOLIAN CAMEL, IS NATIVE TO CENTRAL & EAST ASIA. IT HAS TWO HUMPS, UNLIKE ITS ONE-HUMPED & MORE COMMON RELATIVE, THE DROMEDARY, OR ARABIAN, CAMEL. BACTRIAN CAMELS ARE **BIG** (7 FEET TALL AT THE HUMP), **HEAVY** (1,800 POUNDS), & **TOUGH** (THEY CAN CARRY ABOUT 440 POUNDS ON THEIR BACKS). THEY HAVE ADAPTED TO WITHSTAND THE MONGOLIAN WEATHER, WHICH CAN FALL AS LOW AS −20°F IN WINTER TO ABOVE 100°F IN THE SUMMER, THANKS TO A THICK, SHAGGY COAT THAT FALLS AWAY AS TEMPERATURES INCREASE. THEIR HUMPS STORE FAT, WHICH ENABLES THEM TO GO FOR LONG PERIODS WITHOUT FOOD OR WATER.

THE MONGOLIAN FOOD PYRAMID

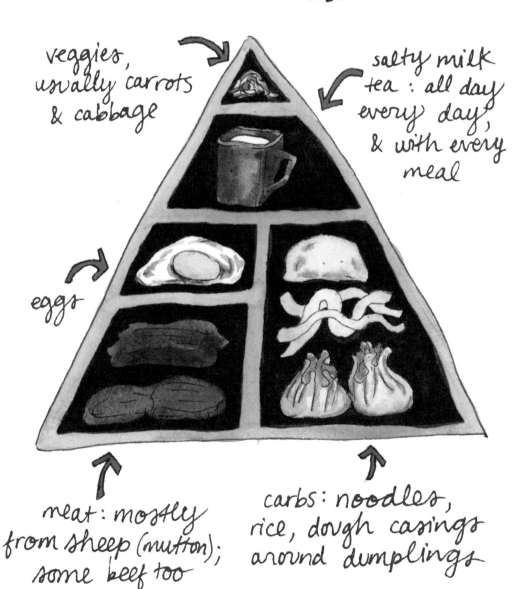

veggies, usually carrots & cabbage

salty milk tea : all day every day, & with every meal

eggs

meat: mostly from sheep (mutton); some beef too

carbs: noodles, rice, dough casings around dumplings

Nomad families move once a season, or 4 times a year, to the same spots. Their diet also changes with the season — here's what they eat:

THE NOMAD DIET

| WINTER "Red Foods" | SPRING FALL | SUMMER "White Foods" |

strips of meat in stews, noodles, soups

BUUZ dumplings with meat

KHUUSHUUR fried meat pockets

AARUUL dried milk curds

KEFIR, MILK

AIRAG fermented mare's milk

LOTS OF MEAT:
EXTREME COLD NECESSITATES HIGHER CALORIC INTAKE. ASIDE FROM SALTY MILK TEA, VERY LITTLE DAIRY IS EATEN: AIRAG & AARUUL ARE CONSUMED SPARINGLY.

ALMOST ENTIRELY DAIRY:
WARM WEATHER = LOWER CALORIC NEEDS. MEAT IS EATEN ONCE DAILY OR NOT AT ALL. AIRAG IS A HUGE SOURCE OF SUSTENANCE, CARRIED ON HORSEBACK IN JUGS.

A MIX OF BOTH RED & WHITE FOODS

dinner with the nomads

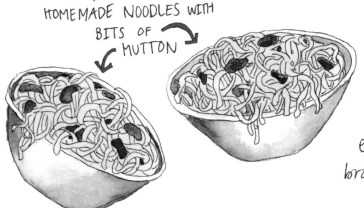

OILY, THICK-CUT HOMEMADE NOODLES WITH BITS OF MUTTON

NOTE: bowls are limited. Pre- & post-meal, you'll drink milk tea out of the same bowl you eat from. Leftover broth is delicious mixed with milk tea!

ORDER OF SERVING: FATHER → GUESTS → MEN → WOMEN → CHILDREN

● ● ● ● ●

WE PASSED THE BOWL OF AIRAG ROUND & ROUND. THE NIGHT WORE ON & EVERYONE GOT WARM & SLEEPY. AROUND 11 PM, THE PARENTS ROSE TO RETURN TO THEIR OWN GER, AND SLEEPING ARRANGEMENTS WERE MADE. HELVIO & I SHARED THE TWIN BED WE'D BEEN SITTING ON ALONG THE WEST (LEFT) SIDE OF THE GER, WHILE THE ELDEST SON & HIS WIFE SLEPT IN A TWIN BED ON THE EAST (RIGHT) SIDE.

March 8, 8 AM

IN THE MORNING, WE AWOKE TO THE ELDEST SON'S WIFE STOKING THE FIRE. WE GOT UP & FOLDED OUR BEDDING, & OUR HOSTESS HANDED US SALTY MILK TEA.

THE ELDEST SON FOLLOWING HIS FATHER OFF TO CHECK ON THE HERDS

The girl & the mother cooked in the ger, and **THE BOY COLLECTED DRIED COW DUNG IN A BASKET.**

WHEN WE STEPPED OUTSIDE, WE DISCOVERED WE WERE THE LAST ONES UP. EVERYONE ELSE IN THE FAMILY WAS WELL INTO THEIR DAY: NOMAD LIFE BEGINS EARLY IN THE MORNING, AROUND 6 AM, AS THERE ARE MANY CHORES TO BE COMPLETED BEFORE NIGHTFALL.

GIFTS EXCHANGED UPON OUR DEPARTURE

GIVING YOUR HOST NOMAD FAMILY TOKEN GIFTS WHEN YOU DEPART IS BOTH KIND & WELCOMED — WE'D READ AS MUCH IN OUR GUIDEBOOK. UNFORTUNATELY, WE WERE NOT AS WELL PREPARED AS WE SHOULD'VE BEEN, PARTLY BECAUSE WE HAD BEEN TRAVELING FOR A WHILE BEFORE BEGINNING THE TRANS-SIBERIAN RAILWAY (WE COULDN'T CARRY ITEMS FROM HOME WITH US IN OUR BACKPACKS FOR MONTHS ON END), & PARTLY BECAUSE WE DID NOT KNOW WHAT WOULD BE APPROPRIATE. WE FEARED GIVING SOMETHING THE FAMILY WOULD FIND STRANGE OR, WORSE, INSULTING. WE WERE EMPTY-HANDED BUT DETERMINED TO GIVE, SO WE GAVE PERSONAL ITEMS: I GAVE THE GIRL MY WATCH, & HELVIO GAVE THE BOY HIS HAT. LATER, I DISCOVERED THAT BATTERIES, PENS, & NOTEBOOKS ARE APPRECIATED GIFTS.

A WOOL HAT *from Helvio to the boy*

A GOLD-TONE WATCH *from me to the girl*

TWO SHAGAI (SHEEP ANKLEBONES) *from the boy to us — I treasure them*

BEFORE WE LEFT, WE TOOK A GROUP PHOTO FOR WHICH EVERYONE (EXCEPT US, OF COURSE) DONNED THEIR FINEST DEELS. WE PACKED UP THE CAR & WERE ON THE ROAD BY ABOUT 10 AM. AS WE DROVE AWAY, THE WOMEN WAVED GOODBYE FROM OUTSIDE THE GER UNTIL THEY WERE SMALL SPECKS IN THE DISTANCE.

IT WAS A BEAUTIFUL DAY, WITH A CLEAR
BLUE SKY & BRIGHT SUN. AS WE DROVE, THE
LANDSCAPE CHANGED FROM SNOWY TO SANDY.
ZORIGOO PUT HIS EXCELLENT OFF-ROAD
DRIVING ON DISPLAY ONCE AGAIN AS
WE TURNED DOWN A SERIES OF SMALLER
DIRT ROADS UNTIL WE WERE DRIVING
ACROSS A DESERT PLAIN TOWARD ANOTHER
GER COMPOUND.

ZORIGOO GAVE THE MAN & WOMAN A WARM GREETING— IT TURNED OUT THEY WERE OLD FRIENDS! THIS WAS A VERY DIFFERENT SITUATION FROM THE DAY BEFORE, WHEN ZORIGOO FOUND THE FAMILY AT RANDOM & WAS HIMSELF AS MUCH A STRANGER TO THE FAMILY AS WE WERE.

ALSO UNLIKE THE LAST NIGHT'S STAY, WHEN WE'D SLEPT IN THE GER WITH THE FAMILY, WE STAYED IN A SEPARATE GUEST GER. ZORIGOO EXPLAINED THAT THE FAMILY HOSTED TOURISTS REGULARLY TO MAKE SOME EXTRA MONEY. WE WERE WELCOMED INTO THE FAMILY'S GER & OFFERED MILK TEA, AIRAG, & SNACKS UPON OUR ARRIVAL.

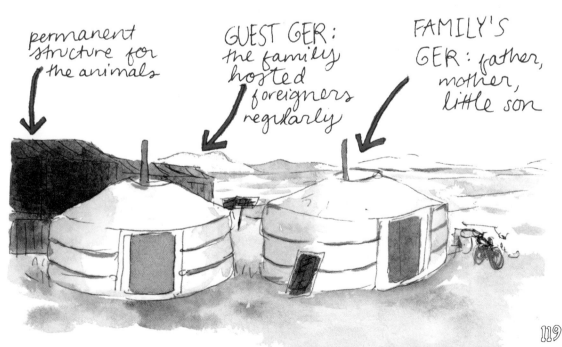

permanent structure for the animals

GUEST GER: the family hosted foreigners regularly

FAMILY'S GER: father, mother, little son

119

KHUURUG

IN MONGOLIA, IT IS CUSTOMARY FOR MEN TO CARRY & EXCHANGE SNUFF FROM _KHUURUG_, OR SNUFF BOTTLES, AS A GESTURE OF FRIENDSHIP & ON SPECIAL OCCASIONS. WHEN WE SAT DOWN FOR TEA, ZORIGOO & HIS FRIEND EXCHANGED SNUFF. ZORIGOO TOOK THE TIME TO EXPLAIN THE RITUAL TO US & OFFERED SNUFF TO BOTH HELVIO & ME TO TRY, ALONG WITH MANY CORRECTIONS PERTAINING TO THE APPROPRIATE WAY TO DO IT.

SNUFF BOTTLE (KHUURUG) EXCHANGE

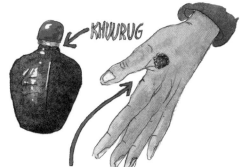

← KHUURUG

SNUFF PLACED HERE

THE BOTTLES ARE PRECIOUS, BEAUTIFUL, & EXPENSIVE! WHEN NOT IN USE, THEY'RE TRANSPORTED IN LITTLE SILK POUCHES.

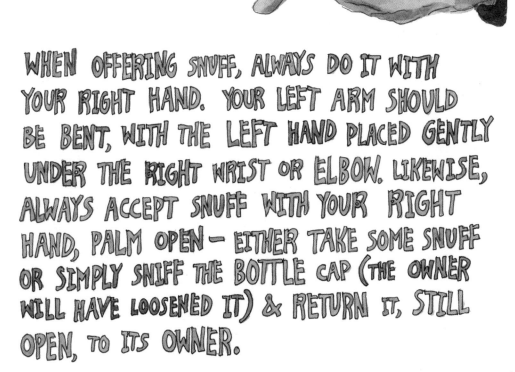

WHEN OFFERING SNUFF, ALWAYS DO IT WITH YOUR RIGHT HAND. YOUR LEFT ARM SHOULD BE BENT, WITH THE LEFT HAND PLACED GENTLY UNDER THE RIGHT WRIST OR ELBOW. LIKEWISE, ALWAYS ACCEPT SNUFF WITH YOUR RIGHT HAND, PALM OPEN — EITHER TAKE SOME SNUFF OR SIMPLY SNIFF THE BOTTLE CAP (THE OWNER WILL HAVE LOOSENED IT) & RETURN IT, STILL OPEN, TO ITS OWNER.

ANAR, THE SON – 5 YEARS OLD. WE BECAME FAST FRIENDS.

AFTER TEA, WE WERE TUGGED OUTSIDE BY GREGARIOUS, ENERGETIC, ALWAYS-GIGGLING ANAR. HE WAS OUR CONSTANT COMPANION & MADE OUR WHOLE STAY BRIGHTER.

to pass the time, we :

RODE CAMELS
the father herded his flocks as we lurched about

TOOK A WALK THROUGH DUNES WITH ANAR, THE MOST _ADORABLE_ GUIDE

DRANK MILK TEA

The family must have had more than 1,000 animals.

March 8, 6 PM

IN THE EVENING, ZORIGOO EXPLAINED THE FAMILY WAS HEADED
TO THE VILLAGE DANCE & THAT WE WERE INVITED. WE WERE VERY
EXCITED ABOUT THE PROSPECT, AS WE HADN'T ANTICIPATED IT. WE
ALSO HAD NO IDEA WHAT TO EXPECT — WE HADN'T READ ANYTHING
ABOUT DANCES IN OUR RESEARCH FOR THE TRIP!

THE NOMAD FAMILY & ZORIGOO CHANGED INTO THEIR FORMAL
DEELS. WE FELT A BIT ASHAMED OF OUR DIRTY BOOTS & UTILITARIAN
CLOTHING, BUT WE GOT INTO THE FAMILY'S CAR & SET OFF FOR
THE COMMUNITY CENTER.

THE DANCE WAS HELD IN A LARGE ROOM WITH CHAIRS LINING 3
OF ITS 4 WALLS, ENOUGH FOR ABOUT 100 PEOPLE TO SIT. AGAINST THE
REMAINING WALL WAS A STAGE WITH MICS & MUSICAL INSTRUMENTS.
THERE WERE ONLY 10 TO 15 PEOPLE WHEN WE ARRIVED, BUT AFTER A FEW
MINUTES THE ROOM STARTED FILLING UP VERY QUICKLY, UNTIL EVERYONE
WAS BUNCHED TOGETHER — WITH HALF THE ATTENDEES SITTING ON ONE
ANOTHER'S LAPS TO MAKE ROOM.

THE ROOM WAS DARK BUT FOR A SERIES OF FLASHING MULTICOLORED
LIGHTS ON THE CEILING — A VERY 1980s NIGHTCLUB VIBE. SOON THE MC
TOOK THE MIC & THERE WAS A SERIES OF PERFORMANCES, MY FAVORITE
OF WHICH WAS A GROUP OF GIRLS WHO DID A TRADITIONAL MONGOLIAN
DANCE SET TO SOME INTENSE ELECTRIC GUITAR.

WHEN THE PERFORMANCES WERE OVER, THE CENTER OF THE ROOM
EMPTIED OUT & THE DJ HIT PLAY. UPBEAT WALTZ MUSIC POURED FROM
THE SPEAKERS, & AROUND THE ROOM'S PERIMETER, PEOPLE JUMPED TO THEIR
FEET TO DANCE WITH FRIENDS & PARTNERS. THE WALTZ SEEMED PRETTY
SIMPLE, SOMETHING BALLROOM DANCERS AROUND THE WORLD WOULD BE
FAMILIAR WITH & PICK UP QUICKLY. DANCING PAIRS SWIRLED AROUND
EACH OTHER AS THE WHOLE GROUP SPUN EN MASSE AROUND THE ROOM
COUNTERCLOCKWISE. A FEW DANCERS ADDED DRAMATIC FLOURISHES,
SOMETIMES CAUSING SMALL TRAFFIC JAMS ON THE CROWDED DANCE FLOOR.

men & women sitting around
the perimeter of the room, watching
the dancers twirl

MARCH 8, 11 PM

HELVIO AND I ARE NOT TALENTED DANCERS, BUT OUR GER HOSTESS INVITED ME TO DANCE FOR THE FIRST SONG SO I GAVE IT A WHIRL. IT DID NOT GO WELL — I HAVE 2 LEFT FEET & I WAS WEARING HUGE EMBARRASSING BOOTS! I MUST HAVE BEEN A FULL HEAD TALLER THAN MOST OF THE ROOM & I FELT VERY MUCH ON DISPLAY WITH MY CLUMSY MOVEMENTS. UNFORTUNATELY, MY BAD DANCING DIDN'T DETER ANYONE — HELVIO & I WERE ASKED TO DANCE FOR EVERY SINGLE DANCE FROM THEN ON. I SENSED THAT THE COMMUNITY DIDN'T WANT US TO FEEL LEFT OUT; I WAS TOUCHED EACH TIME SOMEONE EXTENDED A HAND TO ME WITH A SMILE. I HAVE TROUBLE SAYING NO, SO I CLOMPED AROUND SONG AFTER SONG AS EVERYONE ELSE SWIRLED GRACEFULLY AROUND ME.

The night wore on & the dancing showed no sign of slowing down. Helvio & I were exhausted after our full day of travel, riding camels, & walking around the sand dunes. No doubt most of the nomads in attendance had much more tiring days than us — but we weren't used to life in the steppe! Anar fell asleep on his mom's lap. Zorigoo & his friend dipped out to the car every once in a while to sip on some vodka. We left a bit after midnight, though the dancing was still going strong inside.

MARCH 9, 8am

We woke up & walked over to the family's ger for breakfast. Zorigoo had slept there, & we entered to find him still in bed — it seemed he'd had a late night with his friend! The woman served us breakfast & Anar bounded onto our laps, happy to have his play companions back.

We were supposed to start the multi-hour drive back to Ulaanbaatar as soon as breakfast was done, but it quickly became clear Zorigoo was in no state to get an early start. He nursed his hangover while Helvio & I waited for a few hours outside, playing with Anar. Zorigoo came out after a long while & we began our 3½-hour drive back to Ulaanbaatar.

Back at our guesthouse, we took long, hot showers & had a good night's sleep.

MARCH 10, MORNING

WE STARTED OUR DAY DOWNSTAIRS WITH BREAKFAST & SUUTEI TSAI PROVIDED BY OUR GUESTHOUSE HOSTESS, THEN SET OUT TO SPEND OUR LAST FULL DAY IN MONGOLIA EXPLORING NARANTUUL, ULAANBAATAR'S LARGE OPEN-AIR MARKET.

127

NARANTUUL

THE LARGEST TRADITIONAL MARKET IN THE CITY

НАРАН ТУУЛ ХУДАЛДААНЫ ТӨВ

Inside this turquoise entrance gate is a veritable labyrinth of wares, locally produced & imported. we were sternly warned by our guesthouse host to be wary of pickpockets.

INSIDE NARANTUUL

NARANTUUL IS ENORMOUS! IT'S DIVIDED INTO LARGE SECTIONS, DEPENDING ON THE MERCHANDISE — CLOTHING, FABRIC, FURNITURE, CLEANING SUPPLIES — BUT EVERYTHING IS SOLD BY INDIVIDUAL SELLERS IN STALLS. MANY STALLS SELL IMPORTED GOODS, BUT WE ALSO FOUND SECTIONS WITH TRADITIONAL WARES: BOOTS, TOONOS & OTHER GER-RELATED STRUCTURES, FURNITURE, SADDLES, KHUURUG, & HATS.

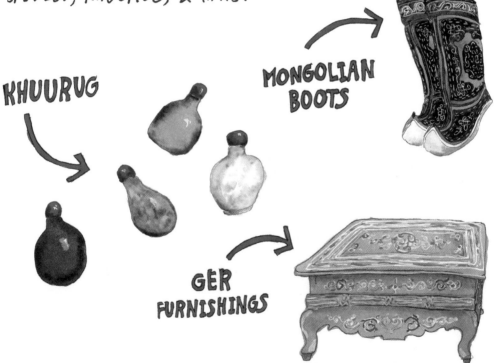

KHUURUG

MONGOLIAN BOOTS

GER FURNISHINGS

the day we went, it was very cold & a bit wet outside; the market was almost deserted. We bought a deck of cards, thinking it might be a nice way to pass the time on the train. I still regret not buying a khuurug as a souvenir.

March 11, morning & afternoon

WE SPENT THE DAY PREPARING FOR OUR DEPARTURE.
WE STUFFED OUR NEW YAK- & CAMEL-WOOL CLOTHES
INTO OUR BACKPACKS AS BEST WE COULD — THANK
GOODNESS FOR COMPRESSION BAGS — & WENT SHOPPING
FOR PROVISIONS. WE WERE READY FOR THE 16-HOUR
TRAIN RIDE TO ULAN-UDE, OUR FIRST DESTINATION
IN RUSSIA.

March 11, 8 PM

FULL OF NEW EXPERIENCES IN MONGOLIA,
WE WERE EXCITED TO GET BACK ON THE TRAIN.
IT WAS EMBLAZONED WITH THE WORDS
"GOLDEN EAGLE TRANS-SIBERIAN EXPRESS,"
WHICH SET THE MOOD QUITE NICELY.

unfortunately, we had two top bunks, but I enjoyed discovering all the ingenious ways things folded away on this train:

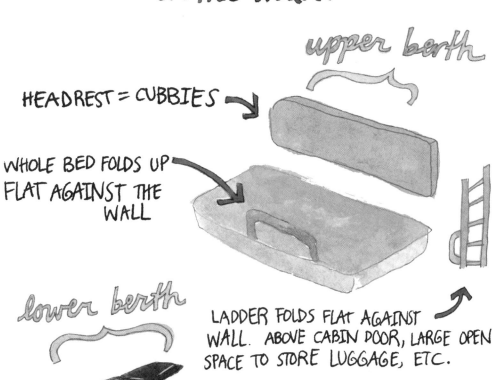

upper berth

HEADREST = CUBBIES →

WHOLE BED FOLDS UP FLAT AGAINST THE WALL

lower berth

LADDER FOLDS FLAT AGAINST WALL. ABOVE CABIN DOOR, LARGE OPEN SPACE TO STORE LUGGAGE, ETC.

HEADRESTS OPEN INTO LITTLE CUBBIES

SEAT OPENS UPWARD TO REVEAL LUGGAGE STORAGE BELOW

WHOLE SEAT BACK FOLDS DOWN TO MAKE BED

131

MARCH 12, 4:30 AM

WE WOKE UP IN SÜHBAATAR, A MONGOLIAN TOWN NEAR THE RUSSIAN BORDER, FOR A MULTI-HOUR CUSTOMS/IMMIGRATION CHECK WITH MONGOLIAN AGENTS.

10:30 AM

WE ARRIVED IN NAUSHKI, THE RUSSIAN BORDER TOWN, FOR MORE OF THE SAME, BUT THIS TIME WITH RUSSIAN BORDER PATROL AGENTS.

I liked her fuzzy hat but not the way she knit her brows at my passport

that's when things went
downhill...

MY RUSSIAN VISA WAS IN MY PREVIOUS
PASSPORT, WHICH HAD RUN OUT OF PAGES, SO
I SHOWED THE VISA (STILL VALID FOR 3 YEARS)
IN MY OLD PASSPORT ALONG WITH MY CURRENT
PASSPORT. WE HAD CROSSED MANY BORDERS
IN OTHER COUNTRIES IN THIS MANNER —
A VISA'S VALIDITY IS SEPARATE
FROM THE PASSPORT'S.

RUSSIA IS ONE OF THE FEW COUNTRIES IN THE WORLD THAT DO NOT ADHERE TO THIS RULE. HERE, YOUR VISA MUST BE IN YOUR CURRENT PASSPORT.

● ● ● ● ●

AT 11 AM, THE BORDER PATROL ESCORTED ME, ALONG WITH MY LUGGAGE,
OFF THE TRAIN. HELVIO HAD TO REMAIN ONBOARD UNTIL THE CUSTOMS &
BORDER CHECK WAS COMPLETE.
   I WAS TAKEN TO A SMALL ANTEROOM JUST OFF THE STATION'S MAIN
WAITING ROOM, WHERE THERE WERE 3 BORDER PATROL AGENTS. I WAS
ASSIGNED A TRANSLATOR, WHO EXPLAINED THAT I HAD BROKEN
RUSSIAN LAW BY ENTERING THE COUNTRY WITHOUT A PROPER VISA.

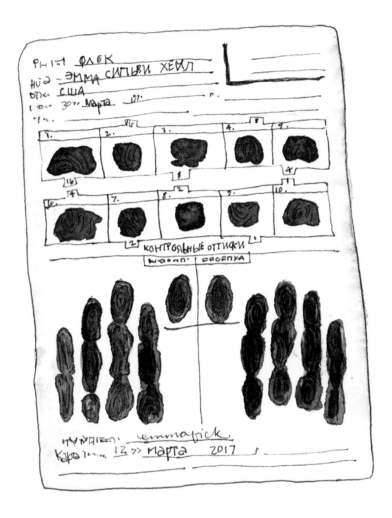

I WAS REQUIRED TO GIVE A POLICE STATEMENT IN WHICH I HAD TO
CONFESS THAT I HAD ENTERED RUSSIA ILLEGALLY. THE TRANSLATOR
REPEATED THE OFFICER'S QUESTIONS IN ENGLISH, THEN WROTE MY ANSWERS
IN RUSSIAN ON THE OFFICIAL DOCUMENTS. I WAS THEN TOLD I WOULD
NEED TO GO BACK TO MONGOLIA ON THE 4 PM TRAIN & OBTAIN A
RUSSIAN VISA WITHIN MY CURRENT PASSPORT. IF I RETURNED TO RUSSIA
I WOULD NEED TO REPORT TO A BANK & PAY A FINE.

THE WHOLE PROCESS TOOK ABOUT AN HOUR. AT NOON, I WAS ALLOWED TO GO OUT TO THE STATION'S OPULENT WAITING ROOM, WHICH WAS PAINTED BUBBLEGUM PINK, LIKE SOMETHING YOU'D SEE IN A WES ANDERSON MOVIE, WITH DECORATIVE FRIEZES COMMEMORATING THE SOVIET ERA RUNNING AROUND THE UPPER PORTION OF THE ROOM'S WALLS.

Soviet-era decorative reliefs

HELVIO WAS WAITING THERE WITH HIS BAGS. I RAN OVER TO HUG HIM. WE SPENT THE NEXT 4 HOURS IN THE PINK WAITING ROOM ATTENDED BY 2 SOMEWHAT SLEEPY OFFICERS WHO PLAYED CHESS TO PASS THE TIME. THE WHOLE EXPERIENCE FELT LIKE A STRANGE ANXIETY DREAM WHERE THINGS-GONE-WRONG MEET THE FANTASTICAL.

OUR MISERABLE JOURNEY
FROM ULAANBAATAR & BACK AGAIN
An hour-by-hour synopsis

DAY 1

MARCH 11
8:35 PM — BOARDED TRAIN, ULAANBAATAR → ULAN-UDE

MARCH 12
4:30 AM — ARRIVED SÜHBAATAR, MONGOLIAN BORDER TOWN. CUSTOMS/IMMIGRATION CHECK BEGAN.

DAY 2

10:30 AM — ARRIVED NAUSHKI, RUSSIAN BORDER TOWN. CUSTOMS/IMMIGRATION CHECK BEGAN.

11 AM — REMOVED FROM TRAIN BY RUSSIAN OFFICIALS. QUESTIONED & FINGERPRINTED.

12-4 PM — WAITED.

4 PM — BOARDED TRAIN BACK TO SÜHBAATAR.

4:40 PM — ARRIVED IN SÜHBAATAR. ENDURED ANOTHER 4-HOUR CUSTOMS/IMMIGRATION CHECK IN WHICH THEY ALMOST CONFISCATED MY CONTACT LENSES.

8:15 PM — CUSTOMS CHECK COMPLETE; ALLOWED TO GET OFF TRAIN. BOUGHT TICKETS TO ULAANBAATAR; ATE DINNER AT RESTAURANT ACROSS THE STREET FROM THE STATION.

8:50 PM — BOARDED TRAIN, SÜHBAATAR → ULAANBAATAR

DAY 3

MARCH 13
5:30 AM — AWOKEN ON TRAIN BY PEOPLE GETTING READY FOR THE DAY.

7:30 AM — ARRIVED BACK IN ULAANBAATAR, EXHAUSTED & DEJECTED.

But that was just the beginning... here's how the rest played out.

The Visa Saga

- 7:30 AM : ARRIVED BACK IN ULAANBAATAR.
- LEFT BAGS AT GUESTHOUSE; WENT IMMEDIATELY TO THE RUSSIAN EMBASSY.
- HOPE: EMBASSY SAID THEY WOULD TRANSFER MY VISA TO MY NEW PASSPORT BUT NEEDED PERMISSION FROM MOSCOW FIRST.

DAY 4 · MARCH 14

- 10 AM : RETURNED TO RUSSIAN EMBASSY.
- DISAPPOINTMENT: NO PROGRESS, VAGUE ANSWERS. EMBASSY'S EMAIL TO MOSCOW RECEIVED NO RESPONSE.
- THEY SAID WE MUST WAIT. SO WE DID.

DAY 5 · MARCH 15

- 9:30 AM : RETURNED TO EMBASSY. NO UPDATES; SHRUGS.

- TEARS: AT THIS POINT, WE'D LOST ABOUT A WEEK OF OUR TRIP & HAD BEGUN TO CONTEMPLATE CATCHING A FLIGHT OUT OF MONGOLIA & GIVING UP OUR TRANS-SIBERIAN JOURNEY ALTOGETHER. THEY TOLD ME THEY'D CALL MOSCOW RIGHT AWAY, & WOULD I _PLEASE_ STOP CRYING.

- 2:00 PM : JOY. MOSCOW APPROVED MY VISA TRANSFER!

DAY 6 · MARCH 16

- 8:00 AM : BOUGHT TRAIN TICKETS AT STATION.
- 12:15 PM : PICKED UP MY VISA/PASSPORT FROM THE RUSSIAN EMBASSY.
- 3:22 PM : ON THE TRAIN TO RUSSIA, NEW VISA IN HAND.

MORAL OF THE STORY: I SHOULD HAVE CRIED SOONER.

Our Itinerary in Russia

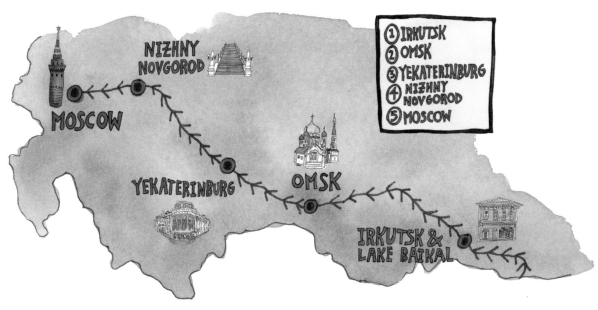

1. IRKUTSK
2. OMSK
3. YEKATERINBURG
4. NIZHNY NOVGOROD
5. MOSCOW

MOSCOW

NIZHNY NOVGOROD

YEKATERINBURG

OMSK

IRKUTSK & LAKE BAIKAL

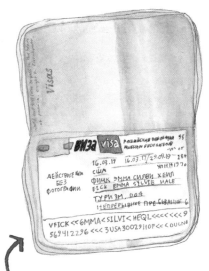

my Russian visa, transferred to my current passport

OUR TICKET to IRKUTSK - WE HAD TO SKIP ULAN-UDE BECAUSE WE HAD LOST TOO MUCH TIME.

my Russian entry stamp

THE SAMOVAR: AN IMPOSSIBLY COMPLICATED CONTRAPTION

the hot water dispenser dripped, & using it was a precarious endeavor on a jostling train, as the water came out boiling hot. There was no cold water.

hallway carpets: blue, with fleur-de-lis

BEDCOVERS: *blue, shabby, with ruffled edges*
BEDS: *very hard mattresses*

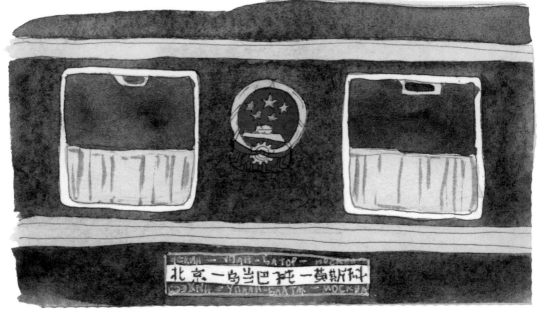

北京 — 乌兰巴托 — 莫斯科

139

ON THIS TRAIN, THE WATER HEATER WAS POWERED BY COAL, SHOVELED BY HAND IN A SOOTY LITTLE ROOM BY THE TRAIN CAR DOOR.

THINGS OBSERVED OUT THE WINDOW BETWEEN LESOVOZNY & SELENGINSK:

KILOMETER MARKERS →

MUCH EASIER TO SEE THAN IN MONGOLIA. THESE INDICATE HOW MANY KILOMETERS YOU ARE FROM MOSCOW, WHICH, THE MOMENT YOU ENTER RUSSIA, BECOMES THE CENTER OF THE UNIVERSE.

← AN EVER-SO-SLIGHTLY VARIED LANDSCAPE THRILLING TO SEE _TREES_ AGAIN!

TIMBER HOUSES WITH POINTY ROOFS, → BROWN
WITH GREEN & BLUE ACCENTS. AESTHETICALLY JARRING: A SHARP DEPARTURE FROM THE SOFT, ROUNDED DOMES OF GERS & FLAT-TOPPED STONE HOUSES OF MONGOLIA.

MOSCOW TIME

IN RUSSIA IN 2017, ALL TRAINS WENT BY MOSCOW TIME.

THIS MEANT THAT NO MATTER WHERE WE WERE OR WHAT TIME ZONE WE WERE IN, ALL THE CLOCKS ON THE TRAIN — AND ALL ARRIVAL/DEPARTURE TIMES DISPLAYED AT TRAIN STATIONS & ON TICKETS — WERE IN UNIVERSAL COORDINATED TIME +3 (UTC+3). ✳

RUSSIA SPANS <u>11</u> TIME ZONES.

TIME ZONE KEY

- ■ KALININGRAD UTC+2
- ■ MOSCOW UTC+3
- ■ SAMARA UTC+4
- ■ YEKATERINBURG UTC+5
- ■ OMSK UTC+6
- ■ KRASNOYARSK UTC+7
- ■ IRKUTSK UTC+8
- ■ YAKUTSK UTC+9
- ■ VLADIVOSTOK UTC+10
- ■ MAGADAN UTC+11
- ■ KAMCHATKA UTC+12

✳ **NOTE:** IN 2018, THIS POLICY CHANGED. NOW LOCAL TIME IS DISPLAYED ON TICKETS & AT TRAIN STATIONS IN ADDITION TO MOSCOW TIME. AND THAT, NO DOUBT, MAKES TRAVELING A LOT LESS CONFUSING!

EXCITING DEVELOPMENT:

made & ate our Mongolia-procured instant soup.

HARD-BOILED EGGS—WHAT LUXURY!—BOUGHT ON THE ULAANBAATAR TRAIN PLATFORM WITH THE LAST OF OUR MONGOLIAN MONEY

we were able to use ALL THREE FUNCTIONS of our sporks!! spoon for broth — fork for noodles — knife for cutting up egg.

to pass the time, we:

WAITED FOR THE BOILING WATER FROM THE DISPENSER TO COOL TO A DRINKABLE ROOM TEMPERATURE

CONTEMPLATED USING THE PLAYING CARDS WE'D BOUGHT FROM NARANTUUL MARKET (for 500₮, or US $0.20) — BUT DIDN'T

ATE FLOWER-FLAVORED BISCUITS

BUILT ENTIRELY of MARBLE!

The two building dates read 1903 & 1909, though most materials I read said the station was completed in 1904.

hammer & sickle

on the platform, slyudyanka

TWO ICE FISHERMEN, ONE WITH A MANUAL ICE AUGER

(THE TOOL FOR DRILLING A HOLE IN THE ICE, TURNED BY HAND — LIKE A GIANT SCREW)

& THE OTHER IN A FUR HAT

SEEING THESE ICE FISHERMEN ON THE PLATFORM WAS A FIRST. THE MANUAL AUGER LOOKED DRAMATIC & ALIEN TO ME — & A LITTLE DANGEROUS! A COUPLE OF DAYS LATER, ON LAKE BAIKAL, I'D SEE ICE FISHING IN MOTION (THOUGH, TO BE HONEST, THERE'S NOT MUCH MOTION INVOLVED).

IN RUSSIA, ICE FISHING IS A NATIONAL PASTIME THAT BORDERS ON AN OBSESSION. FOR RUSSIAN MEN — IT'S ALMOST EXCLUSIVELY MEN WHO INDULGE — THE EXPERIENCE IS ONE OF LEISURE RATHER THAN PRAGMATISM. THE FISH THEMSELVES AREN'T THE POINT. IN FACT, IT'S RARE FOR A FISHERMAN TO CATCH MORE THAN A FEW FISH PER TRIP IN THE WINTER, & THOSE THAT *ARE* CAUGHT ARE GENERALLY SMALL & OF POOR QUALITY. ICE FISHING IS VIEWED MORE AS A SPIRITUAL EXPERIENCE: IT'S ABOUT SOLITUDE, MENTAL CLARITY, & PHYSICAL ENDURANCE. MEN SIT, USUALLY ALONE OR IN PAIRS, ON LOW FOLDING CHAIRS OR STOOLS IN FRONT OF THEIR HOLES. THEY HOLD THEIR LINES, SIP THEIR VODKA, OCCASIONALLY REMOVE ICE CHUNKS FROM THEIR HOLES WITH SLOTTED SPOONS, & CLEAR THEIR HEADS IN THE FRESH, COLD AIR.

I STARTED LOOKING OUT FOR THE ICE FISHERMEN — WITH THEIR GALOSHES, BIG COATS, & ICE AUGERS SLUNG OVER THEIR SHOULDERS, THEY WERE EASY TO SPOT — ON ALL THE SIBERIAN PLATFORMS WHERE WE STOPPED.

145

IRKUTSK

IRKUTSK – THE "PARIS OF SIBERIA" – IS THE MOST POPULAR STOPOVER DESTINATION FOR TOURISTS TAKING THE TRANS-SIBERIAN RAILWAY, PRIMARILY BECAUSE OF ITS PROXIMITY TO LAKE BAIKAL, THE WORLD'S LARGEST FRESHWATER LAKE. IRKUTSK IS THE ECONOMIC CAPITAL OF EASTERN SIBERIA & SINCE ITS FOUNDING IN 1661 HAS BEEN AN IMPORTANT HUB FOR RUSSIA'S TRADE WITH MONGOLIA & CHINA. IN 1879, A FIRE DEVASTATED THE CITY, DESTROYING 75% OF ITS BUILDINGS, ALMOST ALL CONSTRUCTED OF TIMBER IN THE TRADITIONAL SIBERIAN STYLE. VERY FEW OF THOSE CLASSIC SIBERIAN TIMBER HOUSES SURVIVED; TODAY VISITORS CAN SEE THEM HERE & THERE AROUND A THRIVING CITY THAT WAS REBUILT MOSTLY IN STONE.

25 hours later:
WE MADE IT.

*Irkutsk train station,
in yellows & greens*

The long-distance train tickets were sold on the station's second floor in a fabulous light turquoise room with crystal chandeliers.

RUSSIA HAS THE MOST CONSISTENTLY GRANDIOSE & ORNATE PUBLIC TRANSPORT TERMINALS I'VE EVER SEEN.

WE'D ALREADY REVIEWED ALL THE TIMETABLES, SO UPON ARRIVAL IN IRKUTSK WE BOUGHT TICKETS FOR THE NEXT FOUR CITIES ALL AT THE SAME TIME, TO MAKE THINGS EASIER.

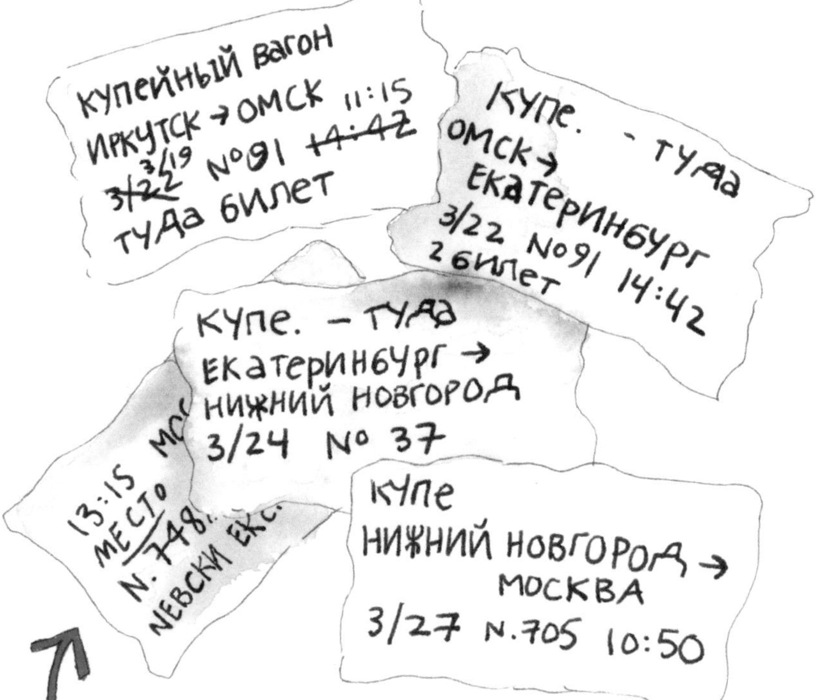

КУПЕЙНЫЙ ВАГОН
ИРКУТСК → ОМСК 11:15
3/19
3/22 №91 14:42
ТУДА БИЛЕТ

КУПЕ. — ТУДА
ОМСК →
ЕКАТЕРИНБУРГ
3/22 №91 14:42
2 БИЛЕТ

КУПЕ. — ТУДА
ЕКАТЕРИНБУРГ →
НИЖНИЙ НОВГОРОД
3/24 № 37

13:15 МО
МЕСТО
N. 748
НЕВСКИ ЕК...

КУПЕ
НИЖНИЙ НОВГОРОД →
МОСКВА
3/27 N.705 10:50

I'd painstakingly copied information—dates, cities, names—in Cyrillic on bits of paper that we passed to the salesclerk.

around Irkutsk

When we arrived at our hostel, we were given a walking map of Irkutsk's "Green Line," which refers to a green line painted on the city sidewalks to guide visitors to its central sites. We set out to cover as much ground as we could before evening. Here are some things we saw:

MONUMENT to THE FOUNDERS of IRKUTSK

ERECTED IN 2011 TO CELEBRATE THE CITY OF IRKUTSK'S 350TH ANNIVERSARY, THIS STATUE OF A COSSACK PIONEER HONORS THOSE WHO FOUNDED THE CITY. THE INSCRIPTION READS: "TO THE FOUNDERS OF IRKUTSK, FROM THE CITIZENS." RUSSIAN FORCES INVADED SIBERIA IN THE LATE 16TH CENTURY; OVER THE NEXT HUNDRED YEARS, RUSSIAN COSSACKS DEFEATED ALLIED TATAR & MONGOLIAN FORCES, ULTIMATELY COLONIZING THE REGION.

LOPSIDED, SLOPING WOODEN HOUSES

FEWER & FEWER OF THESE TRADITIONAL WOODEN HOUSES REMAIN, BUT VISITORS CAN STILL FIND THEM HERE & THERE THROUGHOUT THE CITY. THE BUILDINGS ARE AT ONCE SOLID & DELICATE. THE STRUCTURES ARE MADE FROM ENORMOUS, STURDY LOGS, BUT THE CLASSIC DECORATIVE WOODEN ORNAMENTATION, KNOWN AS LACE, IS ASTONISHINGLY INTRICATE & GIVES AN IMPRESSION OF LIGHTNESS.

THE MOSCOW GATE

ORIGINALLY BUILT IN 1811 BY EMPEROR ALEXANDER I, THIS TRADITIONAL TRIUMPHAL ARCH MARKS THE ENTRANCE TO IRKUTSK FROM THE EUROPEAN PART OF RUSSIA. DESTROYED IN 1928 DURING THE RUSSIAN REVOLUTION DUE TO ITS ASSOCIATION WITH THE MONARCHY, IT WAS REBUILT IN 2011. THE GATE SITS ALONG THE BANK OF THE ANGARA RIVER, WHICH FLOWS FROM LAKE BAIKAL & ULTIMATELY JOINS WITH THE YENISEY RIVER.

CATHEDRAL OF THE EPIPHANY →

OR SOBOR BOGOYAVLENSKY. THIS LANDMARK WAS REBUILT IN 1718 AFTER THE ORIGINAL WOODEN CHURCH BURNED IN 1716. THE ARCHITECTURE IS A FUSION OF RUSSIAN & BAROQUE STYLES.

THE IRKUTSK CIRCUS

THE RUSSIAN CIRCUS TRADITION HAS DEEP ROOTS: THE MODERN ITERATION IS DESCENDED FROM SKOMOROKHI, MEDIEVAL ITINERANT PERFORMERS. OVER THE CENTURIES (THEY WERE FIRST MENTIONED IN LITERARY TEXTS IN THE 11TH CENTURY), SKOMOROKHI PERFORMED AT FOLK FESTIVALS, INCORPORATING SONG, DANCE, COMEDY, & SATIRE INTO THEIR ACTS. THE CIRCUS AS IT IS KNOWN TODAY, PERFORMED IN A RING, WAS ESTABLISHED BY CATHERINE THE GREAT IN THE 19TH CENTURY. TODAY, THE CIRCUS REMAINS A CENTRAL FIXTURE OF RUSSIAN ENTERTAINMENT; MOST CITIES HAVE AN ARENA WHERE BOTH TRAVELING SHOWS & THE CITY'S LOCAL TROUPE CAN PERFORM.

deserted, but for the lone balloon man putting out stuffed animal prizes for the day

AS WE FOLLOWED THE GREEN LINE, I PLAYED I·SPY WITH THE TRADITIONAL WOODEN HOUSES' FOLKLORIC SHUTTERS, EACH MORE FANCIFUL THAN THE LAST.

SIBERIAN SHUTTER SURVEY

MARCH 17, evening

FOR DINNER, WE HAD:
STEWED RABBIT

RASSOLNIK SOUP
WITH SOUR CREAM

DARK
BEER

FRESH-BAKED
RYE BREAD

LIVER STROGANOFF
WITH BUCKWHEAT

153

MARCH 18, *morning*

WE SET OUT FOR <u>TSENTRAL'NYY RYNOK</u>, OR THE CENTRAL MARKET, TO EAT BREAKFAST & EXPLORE. WE ARE MARKET ENTHUSIASTS & TEND TO SEEK THEM OUT EVERYWHERE WE GO: THEY ARE THE PERFECT CONFLUENCE OF TOURISTIC APPEAL & LOCAL UTILITARIANISM, MICROCOSMS OF THE EVERYDAY, CROSSING SOCIOECONOMIC DIVIDES & REVEALING FASCINATING PERSPECTIVES ON A CITY'S PEOPLE & FLAVORS.

A BREAKFAST OF SAVORY PASTRIES, ALL DIPPED IN A RED SAUCE WITH DILL

SMOKED SALMON & CAVIAR GALORE!

ALL KINDS OF SPICES, NUTS, DRIED FRUITS

SMOKED OMUL

old women peddling their jars of preserves

a butcher, his apron bloody, pushing a cart filled with two big slabs of fresh meat

MANY OF THE STALLS WERE POSITIVELY *STUFFED* WITH THEIR WARES. HERE, TOWERS OF CRACKERS - AND THE *TINIEST* LITTLE WINDOW FOR THE WOMAN INSIDE TO PEER OUT & TAKE YOUR ORDER.

OUTSIDE THE MARKET, WE CAUGHT A *MARSHRUTKA* (PUBLIC TRANSPORT MINIVAN) THAT WAS HEADED TO LISTVYANKA, THE CLOSEST VILLAGE ON THE SHORE OF LAKE BAIKAL.

The world's LARGEST, OLDEST, & DEEPEST freshwater lake

LARGEST: CONTAINS ABOUT 20% OF THE WORLD'S FRESH WATER

OLDEST: FORMED ABOUT 25 MILLION YEARS AGO

DEEPEST: 5,387 FEET DEEP

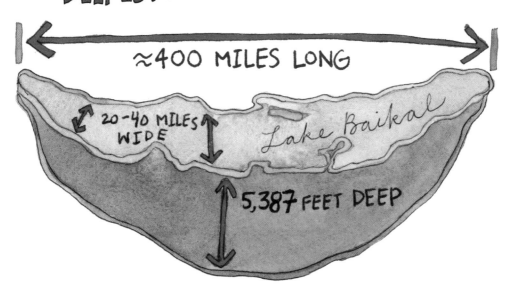

≈400 MILES LONG

20-40 MILES WIDE

Lake Baikal

5,387 FEET DEEP

MANY OF LAKE BAIKAL'S PLANT & ANIMAL SPECIES EVOLVED TO LIVE IN THIS SINGULAR ECOSYSTEM — WHICH INCLUDES, FOR INSTANCE, HIGH LEVELS OF OXYGEN — & CANNOT BE FOUND ANYWHERE ELSE ON EARTH.

SMOKED
(OUR FAVORITE)

SUN-DRIED

omul

OMUL, A MUCH-IN-DEMAND WHITEFISH DELICACY NATIVE TO LAKE BAIKAL, IS THE REGION'S MOST FAMOUS SEAFOOD SPECIALTY. FOR CENTURIES — LONG BEFORE A BOOM IN ITS POPULARITY THROUGHOUT RUSSIA — THIS OILY FISH WAS THE MAIN SOURCE OF FOOD FOR THOSE WHO LIVED AROUND THE LAKE. TODAY, OMUL IS BELOVED & SOUGHT AFTER THROUGHOUT THE COUNTRY (AFTER IT'S SMOKED, IT'S EASILY TRANSPORTED). TRYING FRESH OMUL WAS AT THE TOP OF OUR LIST WHEN WE VISITED BAIKAL: WE WERE ENTHUSIASTIC ABOUT THE OPPORTUNITY TO EAT SOMETHING THAT WE LITERALLY COULD NOT TASTE ANYWHERE ELSE ON EARTH!

THE FLAVOR OF OMUL, OILY & RICH, DID NOT DISAPPOINT, BUT THE FISH'S POPULARITY COMES AT A PRICE. IN LATE 2017, RUSSIA IMPOSED A 3-YEAR BAN ON COMMERCIAL OMUL FISHING DUE TO TROUBLING POPULATION DECLINE, LIKELY FROM A COMBINATION OF OVERFISHING, CLIMATE CHANGE, & ALGAE BLOOMS IN THE LAKE CAUSED BY WASTE DUMPING. THE FISHING BAN IS NOT UNPRECEDENTED: IN 1969, A 10-YEAR OMUL FISHING BAN WAS IMPOSED DUE TO SIMILAR POPULATION DECLINE CONCERNS, & WAS EFFECTIVE IN RESTORING THE POPULATION TO HEALTHY NUMBERS.

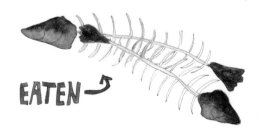

EATEN

LISTVYANKA

THE MARSHRUTKA FROM IRKUTSK TO LISTVYANKA WAS ABOUT AN HOUR'S JOURNEY. THE VAN DROPPED US OFF IN FRONT OF THE CLOSED TOURIST OFFICE IN LISTVYANKA, WHICH LOOKED OUT DRAMATICALLY OVER THE FROZEN LAKE. WE SET OUT ON FOOT TO THE HOTEL ROOM WE'D BOOKED THE PREVIOUS NIGHT.

OUR NO-FRILLS LOG CABIN HOTEL WAS UP A LITTLE HILL

THE WALK UP THE ICY DIRT PATH WAS TREACHEROUS, BUT AT LEAST WE GOT TO ENJOY THE ADORABLE, OFTEN LOPSIDED WOODEN HOUSES WITH THEIR TRADITIONAL WINDOWS.

MARCH 18, afternoon

AFTER WE CHECKED INTO OUR ROOM,
WE WANDERED DOWN TO THE LAKE,
ADMIRING THE ARCHITECTURE ALONG
THE WAY. IT MAY HAVE BEEN COLD
& GRAY OUTSIDE, BUT WINDOWS
THROUGHOUT LISTVYANKA OFFERED
GLIMPSES INTO A WARM & BRIGHT
INTERIOR LIFE.

↰ plant-filled windowsills with
floral-patterned lace curtains

ways to get around the lake

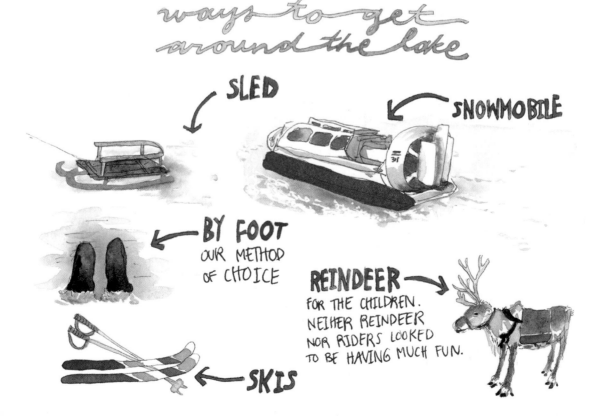

SLED

SNOWMOBILE

BY FOOT
OUR METHOD
OF CHOICE

REINDEER
FOR THE CHILDREN.
NEITHER REINDEER
NOR RIDERS LOOKED
TO BE HAVING MUCH FUN.

SKIS

159

AT THE OMUL MARKET,

LOCATED ON LISTVYANKA'S MAIN ROAD, WHICH RUNS PARALLEL TO & OVERLOOKS THE LAKE, EVERY VENDOR WAS SELLING THE SAME THING: OMUL. AS WE PASSED, EACH VENDOR ROSE FROM THEIR SEAT & OPENED A BOX OF FISH. THE HOT STEAM PUFFED OUT DRAMATICALLY INTO THE COLD AIR, TRAILING BEHIND US AS WE WALKED, AS IF WE WERE ROYALTY MAKING SOME GRAND ENTRANCE.

All the fish looked identical to us — how were we possibly supposed to choose between the dozens of vendors?

WE ARBITRARILY CHOSE SOME OMUL TO EAT (FRESH-SMOKED, NOT DRIED).

WE ALSO PICKED UP SOME OF THE UBIQUITOUS LOAVES OF FLAT-YET-PUFFY BREAD, WARM & SOFT, FROM ONE OF THE BREAD VENDORS WHO FLANKED THE MARKET ENTRANCE.

OMUL + WARM FRESH BREAD = HEAVEN

WE WALKED ON THE
LAKE & ATE OMUL. THERE REALLY WASN'T
MUCH ELSE TO DO — *and that*
was just fine.

dry, powdery
snow on the surface
of the ice, making
windblown patterns
just like sand on
a beach

little windows into
the lake itself where
the snow had blown away,
revealing webs of deep
cracks in the ice, which
freezes up to 6½ feet
thick in the winter

At Lake Baikal that afternoon, we wandered about & discovered that the side roads of the village had the best omul offerings, <u>NOT</u> the central market.

MARCH 19, 7 AM

After a cozy night in our log cabin attic room, we bundled up & headed down to the lake with a thermos of instant coffee. We spent an hour sipping coffee & walking on the ice before eating breakfast: one last smoked omul. We had to! It was our last chance!

9 AM

Full of icy vistas & omul, we caught the marshrutka back to Irkutsk.

Goodbye, Baikal.

The marshrutka dropped us off outside the central market in Irkutsk, & from there we caught a taxi to the railway station for our train's 11:15am departure to Omsk.

on the train
IRKUTSK → OMSK

AN *EXTREMELY* CLEAN & WELL-FURBISHED TRAIN

← maroon carpet

thick, soft camel-colored blankets; crisp white sheets

blue seats below, beige above; reading lights provided

TV above the cabin door (a first!) — had about 3 channels, all Russian soap operas

AROUND 5:30 PM, WE WERE BAFFLED WHEN TWO CARDBOARD BOXES WERE DELIVERED TO US BY A WOMAN WITH A ROLLING CART & ZERO PATIENCE FOR OUR INABILITY TO SPEAK RUSSIAN.

inside each box: some truly terrible food

(apparently included with our ticket

SOGGY ELBOW MACARONI & A PALE BROWN MEAT IN SAUCE

COOKIE WITH A LITTLE TRAIN ON IT

BOTTLE OF WATER

TWO PIECES OF PARTLY STALE BREAD

WE SHARED OUR *KUPÉ* (RUSSIAN WORD FOR A COUCHETTE/SECOND-CLASS CABIN) WITH A SWEET, MELLOW MIDDLE-AGED RUSSIAN COUPLE.
THEY LIKED:

standing in the hallway & looking out the windows. They liked this most of all.

playing sudoku & other puzzles from the little stack of booklets they brought

drinking tea from <u>PODSTAKANNIKI</u>, the classic Russian tea glass holders. The metal base converts a regular drinking glass to a cup with a handle so you can drink a hot beverage more safely, especially on a jostling train. Though they're no longer prevalent in Russian homes, podstakanniki remain popular on trains because the base is so stable. If you order tea on the train, it'll be served in a podstakannik, & you can even buy one from your <u>provodnitsa</u> (train attendant) to keep as a souvenir.

FROM THE TOP BUNK,
I WATCHED OUR KUPÉ-MATES
BELOW DRINK BLACK TEA FROM
PODSTAKANNIKI. THIS STRUCK
ME AS AN UNEXPECTEDLY INTIMATE
SCENE.

The landscape was still largely snow, trees (birch & evergreens, most notably), & Siberian wooden houses with their blue & green (& sometimes yellow or red) accents.

WE WANDERED THROUGH THE LINKED TRAIN CARS
TO STRETCH OUR LEGS. WE FOUND THE CABOOSE & SPENT
SOME TIME WATCHING THE TRACKS UNSPOOL BEHIND US.

THE RUSSIAN DINING CAR

LOUD DRAPES,
FUTURISTIC SEATS, & A GRUMPY SERVER

we ordered :

"SANDWICH WITH SMOKED SAUSAGE COOKED"

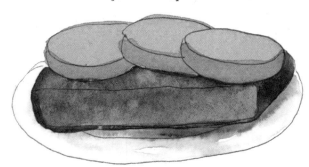

DESCRIBED AS "WHITE BREAD, SAUSAGE SMOKED-COOKED, CUCUMBER, HERBS,"
IT WAS SO SMALL IT FIT INTO THE PALM OF MY HAND.
CUCUMBER & HERBS WERE <u>NOT</u> INCLUDED.

BORSCHT

VERY SMALL & VERY EXPENSIVE.

A GENERALLY ACCEPTED*
RANKING of the
VARIOUS DINING CARS

(ALL SECOND-CLASS; NO FIRST-CLASS EXPERIENCE)

+ CHINESE CAR

simple stir fries, rice dishes.
Tasty, filling, & good prices.

BETTER

+ MONGOLIAN CAR

limited options, basic fare —
but tasty & prices were okay.

ALL WERE PRETTY GOOD, & DEFINITELY WORTHWHILE EXPERIENCES.

+ RUSSIAN CAR

lots of options (not all available)
but florid descriptions made way
for meager portions. Not very
tasty & expensive.

WORSE

* JUST JOKING. THIS IS MY HIGHLY SUBJECTIVE OPINION BASED ON VERY LIMITED DATA, LARGELY UNFOUNDED, & CERTAINLY CONTROVERSIAL.

AT 38 HOURS, THE JOURNEY FROM IRKUTSK TO OMSK WAS
THE LONGEST CONTINUOUS STRETCH OF TIME WE SPENT ON
THE TRAIN. WE WERE LUCKY TO HAVE QUIET & COURTEOUS
KUPÉ-MATES, & THE TIME PASSED PLEASANTLY ENOUGH. SINCE WE
DIDN'T HAVE THE WINDOW SEATS IN OUR KUPÉ — THE WOES OF
THE UPPER BERTH! — WE SPENT MORE TIME ON THIS LEG OF
THE TRIP READING & LISTENING TO PODCASTS. WE OFTEN HUNG
OUT ON OUR BEDS, WHICH FELT PRIVATE. THE WHOLE TRAIN
WAS WARM — A BIT TOO WARM FOR MY COMFORT — & OUR
MANY LAYERS & JACKETS HUNG UNTOUCHED BY THE DOOR. WE
WERE IN SHORT SLEEVES EVEN THOUGH THE SNOW WAS THICK
OUTSIDE OUR WINDOW.

OMSK

ВОКЗАЛ

38 HOURS LATER:
WE ARRIVED AROUND
MIDNIGHT.

OUR REASONS FOR VISITING OMSK WERE PRACTICAL. UNLIKE
IRKUTSK, AN EXTREMELY POPULAR TOURIST DESTINATION, OMSK IS
NOT BILLED AS A PARTICULARLY APPEALING CITY FOR VISITORS.
WE ELECTED TO STOP AT THIS INDUSTRIAL SIBERIAN METROPOLIS
BECAUSE ITS TRAIN DEPARTURE DATES ALIGNED BEST WITH OUR PLAN
TO MOVE ON TO YEKATERINBURG. I DO ENJOY STOPPING AT
NONTOURISTIC CITIES: VISITING A THRIVING, WORKING-CLASS SIBERIAN
CITY BALANCED THE TOURISTIC OVERTONES OF LAKE BAIKAL NICELY.

Our hostel in Omsk — named "DOSTOYEVSKY" because the writer spent 4 years in prison here — was located across the tracks from the train station, easily reached by a pedestrian bridge that afforded great views over the crisscrossing rails.

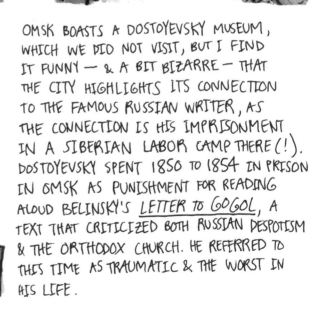

FYODOR DOSTOYEVSKY

OMSK BOASTS A DOSTOYEVSKY MUSEUM, WHICH WE DID NOT VISIT, BUT I FIND IT FUNNY — & A BIT BIZARRE — THAT THE CITY HIGHLIGHTS ITS CONNECTION TO THE FAMOUS RUSSIAN WRITER, AS THE CONNECTION IS HIS IMPRISONMENT IN A SIBERIAN LABOR CAMP THERE (!). DOSTOYEVSKY SPENT 1850 TO 1854 IN PRISON IN OMSK AS PUNISHMENT FOR READING ALOUD BELINSKY'S LETTER TO GOGOL, A TEXT THAT CRITICIZED BOTH RUSSIAN DESPOTISM & THE ORTHODOX CHURCH. HE REFERRED TO THIS TIME AS TRAUMATIC & THE WORST IN HIS LIFE.

OUR HOSTEL BED SURE FELT NICE AFTER A NIGHT ON THE TRAIN. WE FIXED OURSELVES A SIMPLE BREAKFAST IN THE HOSTEL KITCHEN WITH THE DREGS OF OUR IRKUTSK MARKET FOOD & CHATTED WITH THE ONLY OTHER GUEST THAT NIGHT, A YOUNG MAN FROM KAZAKHSTAN WHO WAS LIVING THERE LONG-TERM. WE MAPPED OUT OUR ITINERARY FOR OUR ONE FULL DAY IN OMSK.

OUR ITINERARY:

- A VISIT TO DORMITION CATHEDRAL
- A WANDER AROUND THE CITY CENTER
- AND, AS ALWAYS, A STOP AT THE CENTRAL MARKET (WE HAD TO STOCK UP ON MORE FOOD FOR THE TRAIN ANYWAY)

THE TICKET COLLECTOR, READING. HER DESIGNATED SEAT, MARKED WITH A SIGN, WAS COVERED IN A THICK CARPET.

SHE WANTED TO KNOW WHERE WE WERE GOING, HAD US SIT BY HER, AND VERY HELPFULLY MADE SURE WE GOT OFF AT THE RIGHT STOP.

DORMITION CATHEDRAL,
USPENSKIY KAFEDRAL'NYY SOBOR

ORIGINALLY BUILT AT THE END OF THE 19TH CENTURY, DORMITION CATHEDRAL IS ONE OF THE LARGEST RUSSIAN ORTHODOX CHURCHES IN SIBERIA. IT WAS DESTROYED IN THE 1930s, THEN RESTORED TO ITS ORIGINAL STATE IN 2007. TODAY, IT'S A STRIKING VISION IN THE MIDDLE OF DOWNTOWN OMSK. BECAUSE IT SITS IN THE CENTER OF A LARGE SQUARE, ONE CAN APPRECIATE ITS WHIMSICAL ARCHITECTURE & VIBRANT COLORS FROM ALL SIDES.

AFTER A FRESH SNOWFALL, THE GROUND AROUND THE SQUARE GLIMMERED WHITE, & THE CATHEDRAL ROSE DRAMATICALLY, GOLD ONION TOPS GLINTING IN THE BRIGHT SUNLIGHT. I FELT LIKE ALL THE ILLUSTRATED FAIRY TALES FROM MY CHILDHOOD WERE MATERIALIZING BEFORE MY EYES. WE CIRCLED THE CATHEDRAL & SAT ON BENCHES TO TAKE IT IN FROM VARIOUS ANGLES.

INSIDE, ROTUND MATRONS IN VESTS & HAIR KERCHIEFS WASHED THE FOREHEAD & KISS MARKS FROM THE ICONS' PROTECTIVE GLASS WITH FREQUENCY.

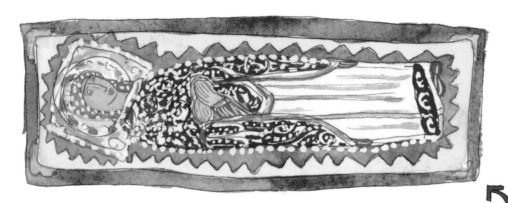

Inside Dormition Cathedral, I especially loved this embroidered depiction of Mary's dormition (her earthly death, before her assumption to heaven).

I was also taken with this icon depicting Saint Olga, who holds a church in her arms (the church represents her role in bringing Christianity to Russia in the 10th century).

IN OMSK, WE DISCOVERED THE JOY THAT IS THE *STOLOVAYA.*

THE RUSSIAN **STOLOVAYA**

in Cyrillic:

СТОЛОВАЯ

THE LITERAL TRANSLATION IS "CANTEEN," BUT I THINK A BETTER WORD TO DESCRIBE IT IS "CAFETERIA." **CHEAP, DELICIOUS, SIMPLE, TRADITIONAL RUSSIAN FOOD.**

VERY SALT-OF-THE-EARTH. (WHAT MORE COULD YOU WANT?!)

Grab a plastic tray & slide it along the metal rails in front of the glass cases of food.

THERE ARE *TWO* TYPES OF STOLOVAYA:

① THE FOOD IS PRE-PORTIONED IN LITTLE DISHES (as pictured) FOR YOU TO TAKE, OR

② THERE ARE SERVERS WHO STAND BEHIND THE GLASS AND *THEY* SERVE THE PORTION OF WHATEVER YOU WANT ON A PLATE.

A TYPICAL END RESULT OF THE *SERVER-STYLE* STOLOVAYA: ONE BIG PLATE WITH MAINS, ONE OR TWO SMALLER PLATES WITH SIDES/SOUPS

VS.

A TYPICAL END RESULT OF THE *PRE-PORTIONED-STYLE* STOLOVAYA: A MILLION SMALL PLATES, STACKED PRECARIOUSLY

STOLOVAYAS BEGAN AS GOVERNMENT-RUN EATERIES IN THE 1920s. THEY WERE PART OF THE POST REVOLUTION COMMUNIST ETHOS THAT EVERYONE DESERVED TO BE ABLE TO EAT. THOUGH THEY'VE CHANGED OVER THE YEARS, AFFORDABLE, NO-FRILLS FOOD HAS REMAINED A CONSTANT.

At our first stolovaya, we ate:

BORSCHT WITH A DOLLOP OF SOUR CREAM

CARROT & CABBAGE SALAD

CHEESY SALMON ON A BED OF BUCKWHEAT

BEET SALAD

BLACK TEA

HERRING UNDER A FUR COAT

I FELL IN LOVE WITH THIS DISH AT A STOLOVAYA BEFORE KNOWING WHAT IT WAS CALLED, & WHEN I LEARNED ITS NAME I COMPLETELY LOST MY MIND. IT TASTED _EVEN BETTER_ WHEN I COULD SAVOR ITS HILARIOUS NAME ALONG WITH ITS FLAVOR!

CRUMBLED HARD-BOILED EGG

BEETS & MAYONNAISE

STEAMED POTATOES, CARROTS

SALT-CURED HERRING

NOT FOR THE FAINT OF TASTE BUDS. THE INGREDIENT-LAYER ORDER MAY VARY, AND EGG GARNISH IS OPTIONAL.

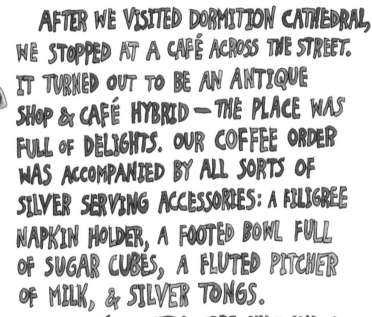

AFTER WE VISITED DORMITION CATHEDRAL, WE STOPPED AT A CAFÉ ACROSS THE STREET. IT TURNED OUT TO BE AN ANTIQUE SHOP & CAFÉ HYBRID — THE PLACE WAS FULL OF DELIGHTS. OUR COFFEE ORDER WAS ACCOMPANIED BY ALL SORTS OF SILVER SERVING ACCESSORIES: A FILIGREE NAPKIN HOLDER, A FOOTED BOWL FULL OF SUGAR CUBES, A FLUTED PITCHER OF MILK, & SILVER TONGS.

THE CAFÉ OWNERS WERE HUSBAND & WIFE. THEY SPOKE TO US IN RAPID RUSSIAN EVEN AFTER WE GESTURED THAT WE COULDN'T UNDERSTAND A

THING. I LIKE TO THINK WE ABSORBED INFORMATION IN SPITE OF THE LANGUAGE BARRIER — AND WE CERTAINLY ABSORBED THEIR KINDNESS & GENEROSITY.

THERE WERE SILVER SAMOVARS & OLD PENDULUM CLOCKS SURROUNDING THE TABLE WHERE WE SAT. WHEN WE EXPRESSED INTEREST IN THE CLOCKS, THE HUSBAND SET ALL THE PENDULUMS SWINGING, UNTIL WE WERE SURROUNDED BY A SYMPHONY OF TICKING.

Brightly painted wooden Siberian houses can be found here & there around the city center. Sandwiched between modern buildings, they look like forgotten toys.

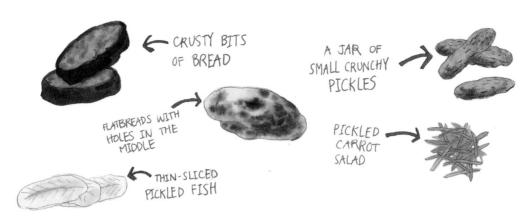

CRUSTY BITS OF BREAD

A JAR OF SMALL CRUNCHY PICKLES

FLATBREADS WITH HOLES IN THE MIDDLE

PICKLED CARROT SALAD

THIN-SLICED PICKLED FISH

march 21, evening

AFTER STOCKING UP ON SOME MORE TRAIN SNACKS FOR THE RIDE TO YEKATERINBURG, WE SPENT OUR SECOND & FINAL NIGHT IN OMSK THOROUGHLY ENJOYING OUR QUEEN-SIZE BED AT DOSTOYEVSKY HOSTEL. WE SLEPT WELL THAT NIGHT KNOWING IT WAS ONLY A 5-MINUTE WALK TO THE TRAIN STATION.

Travel tip: when it comes to lodging, we prioritized proximity to the train station over proximity to the touristic city center. That way, when we arrived in a city we could drop off our bags without having to navigate public transportation or get a taxi with our bulky loads. On the way back to the train station for departure, we liked not having to worry about a late bus or traffic jam that might cause us to miss our train.

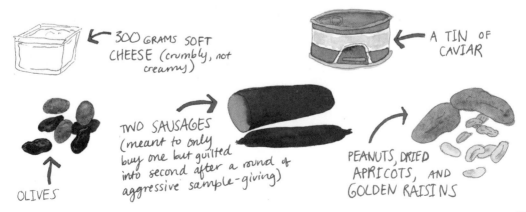

300 GRAMS SOFT CHEESE (crumbly, not creamy)

A TIN OF CAVIAR

TWO SAUSAGES (meant to only buy one but guilted into second after a round of aggressive sample-giving)

OLIVES

PEANUTS, DRIED APRICOTS, AND GOLDEN RAISINS

BACK ON THE TRAIN

march 22, 5:20 PM

NEXT STOP: <u>YEKATERINBURG</u>, THE LAST CITY WE'D VISIT IN "ASIAN RUSSIA" BEFORE WE CROSSED THE URAL MOUNTAINS TO ENTER "EUROPEAN RUSSIA." COMPARED TO OUR PREVIOUS TRAVEL TIMES, THE 12-HOUR JOURNEY FROM OMSK TO YEKATERINBURG WAS A MERE BLIP, ESPECIALLY BECAUSE WE WERE TRAVELING THROUGH THE NIGHT. WE SLEPT MOST OF THE WAY.

THE URAL MOUNTAINS SERVE AS THE GEOGRAPHICAL BOUNDARY BETWEEN EUROPEAN RUSSIA & ASIAN RUSSIA (AKA *SIBERIA*).

THE URAL MOUNTAINS

●MOSCOW

●YEKATERINBURG

RUSSIA

Siberia

■ EUROPEAN RUSSIA
□ URAL MOUNTAINS
■ ASIAN RUSSIA

YEKATERINBURG, THE FOURTH-LARGEST CITY IN RUSSIA, IS THE DE FACTO CAPITAL OF THE URALS, THE MOUNTAIN RANGE THAT STRETCHES ACROSS RUSSIA FROM NORTH (THE ARCTIC OCEAN) TO SOUTH (KAZAKHSTAN).

IT'S ALSO OF HISTORICAL NOTE: THE RUSSIAN IMPERIAL ROMANOV FAMILY (EMPEROR NIKOLAI II & EMPRESS ALEXANDRA, ALONG WITH THEIR 5 CHILDREN) WAS ASSASSINATED BY THE BOLSHEVIKS HERE IN JULY 1918, & BORIS YELTSIN, THE FIRST PRESIDENT OF THE RUSSIAN FEDERATION, WAS BORN IN BUTKA, A NEARBY VILLAGE.

THE ROMANOVS

BORIS YELTSIN

Train Fashion

COMFORT ABOVE ALL ELSE. WE NOTICED THAT MANY RUSSIAN TRAVELERS WOULD CHANGE FROM STREET CLOTHES TO COMFORT CLOTHES IMMEDIATELY AFTER GETTING ON THE TRAIN. THIS WOMAN PROMPTLY CHANGED INTO THIS OUTFIT:

FLOWERED HEADBAND

PLAID SHIRT

FLOWERED SHORTS

FUZZY SLIPPERS

This train interior was not our favorite: no carpet in the hallway & faux wood everywhere we looked.

YEKATERINBURG

march 23, afternoon

YEKATERINBURG IS HOME TO A NUMBER OF MUSEUMS, BUT SINCE WE ONLY HAD A DAY & A HALF TO EXPLORE, WE ELECTED TO WALK FAR & WIDE INSTEAD. THIS BUILDING ON THE BANK OF THE ISET RIVER— BUILT BY A WEALTHY MERCHANT NAMED SEVASTYANOV IN THE 19TH CENTURY — WAS OUR FAVORITE PIECE OF ARCHITECTURE.

The Sevastyanov House

Walking the Yekaterinburg streets, we were struck by a clear sign — visually, & in some intangible way culturally too — that we were leaving Asia & entering Europe.

RELIEF OF THE FOUNDERS OF YEKATERINBURG

THIS RELIEF SITS ABOVE THE DAM ON THE ISET RIVER IN THE CITY CENTER. THE MAN SITTING WITH A LARGE PIECE OF PAPER ON A DESK, HOLDING WHAT LOOKS TO BE A COMPASS, IS VASILY TATISHCHEV, ONE OF THE RUSSIAN STATESMEN WHO FOUNDED YEKATERINBURG IN 1723. THE PLAQUE IN FRONT READS: "_GLORIOUS SONS OF RUSSIA V.N. TATISHCHEV & W. DE GENNIN, YEKATERINBURG IS THANKFUL, 1998._"

LENIN STATUE IN 1905 SQUARE

FOR ME, SPOTTING LENIN EVERYWHERE WAS THE EQUIVALENT OF SEEING CHINGGIS KHAAN IN MONGOLIA. HE'S ALL OVER THE PLACE! MANY CITY SQUARES FEATURE LENIN STATUES. SIMILAR TO CHINGGIS KHAAN, MUCH OF THE WORLD DEPICTS LENIN AS A VILLAIN, BUT IN HIS HOME COUNTRY HIS LEGACY IS QUITE POSITIVE.

VLADIMIR ILYICH ULYANOV — WHO LATER ADOPTED THE PSEUDONYM LENIN, THE NAME BY WHICH HE'S KNOWN WORLD-WIDE TODAY — WAS BORN IN 1870 IN SIMBIRSK (NOW ULYANOVSK), A CITY ABOUT 500 MILES EAST OF MOSCOW. HE CAME FROM A HIGHLY CULTURED, EDUCATED FAMILY, & THEY EXPERIENCED THE AUTOCRACY'S EFFORTS TO CURB PUBLIC EDUCATION AS WELL AS DENY CIVIL RIGHTS TO THE EDUCATED. LENIN WAS FIRST SPURRED INTO REVOLUTIONARY ACTION IN 1887, WHEN HIS OLDER BROTHER, A STUDENT AT THE UNIVERSITY OF SAINT PETERSBURG, WAS EXECUTED FOR BEING PART OF A GROUP PLOTTING TO ASSASSINATE TSAR ALEXANDER III. LENIN ENTERED UNIVERSITY JUST A FEW MONTHS AFTER HIS BROTHER'S DEATH; HE WAS EXPELLED 4 MONTHS LATER FOR TAKING PART IN A STUDENT PROTEST.

LENIN EVENTUALLY FINISHED HIS EDUCATION, THEN PRACTICED AS A DEFENSE ATTORNEY FOR A FEW YEARS IN THE MID-1890s. AS A UNIVERSITY STUDENT, LENIN FOUND THE WORKS OF COMMUNIST THINKER KARL MARX, & IN 1894 PENNED HIS FIRST MARXIST ESSAY. SOON AFTER, HE WAS ARRESTED FOR WORKING ON A MARXIST NEWSPAPER & EXILED TO A SIBERIAN PRISON UNTIL 1900.

UPON HIS RELEASE FROM PRISON, LENIN WENT TO WESTERN EUROPE TO CONVENE WITH LIKE-MINDED MARXIST THINKERS. DURING THESE YEARS ABROAD, HE ADOPTED THE PSEUDONYM LENIN & ESTABLISHED THE BOLSHEVIK PARTY, FOUNDED ON REVOLUTIONARY FAR-LEFT MARXIST VALUES.

LENIN RETURNED TO RUSSIA IN 1917 &, WITH THE BACKING OF THE GERMAN GOVERNMENT, LED THE OCTOBER REVOLUTION— ALSO KNOWN AS THE BOLSHEVIK COUP — THAT YEAR, EFFECTIVELY ENDING TSARIST RULE IN RUSSIA. A BLOODY CIVIL WAR FOLLOWED, WITH THE LENIN-BACKED RED ARMY ULTIMATELY BEATING THE WHITE ARMY. IN 1922, THE UNION OF SOVIET SOCIALIST REPUBLICS (USSR) WAS FORMED, WITH LENIN AS ITS FIRST LEADER.

LENIN BECAME ILL JUST MONTHS LATER. IN AN APRIL 1922 SURGERY, A BULLET FROM AN ASSASSINATION ATTEMPT WAS PULLED FROM HIS NECK, & WHILE HE RECOVERED INITIALLY, AFTER THAT HE SUFFERED BOUTS OF SEMIPARALYSIS, LOSS OF SPEECH, & STROKES, THE LAST OF WHICH ENDED HIS LIFE IN 1924 AT THE AGE OF 54. UNLIKE HIS SUCCESSOR, JOSEPH STALIN, WHOSE LIKENESS HAS LARGELY BEEN SCRUBBED FROM PUBLIC SPACES IN RUSSIA — HIS FACE REMOVED FROM MURALS, HIS NAME REMOVED FROM STREETS & BUILDINGS — LENIN'S CULT OF PERSONALITY REMAINS STRONG, THOUGH SIGNIFICANTLY DIMINISHED SINCE ITS PEAK IN THE 1970s. EVEN IF HE'S NOT WORSHIPPED WITH THE SAME FERVOR TODAY, HIS PRESENCE REMAINS UBIQUITOUS: LENIN STATUES LOOK DOWN ON PASSERSBY THE WHOLE COUNTRY OVER, STREETS & SQUARES BEAR HIS NAME IN ALMOST EVERY CITY, & HIS EMBALMED BODY REMAINS IN THE CENTER OF MOSCOW, RIGHT NEXT TO THE KREMLIN, WITH LINES OF VIEWERS WAITING TO PAY THEIR RESPECTS DAILY.

LENIN

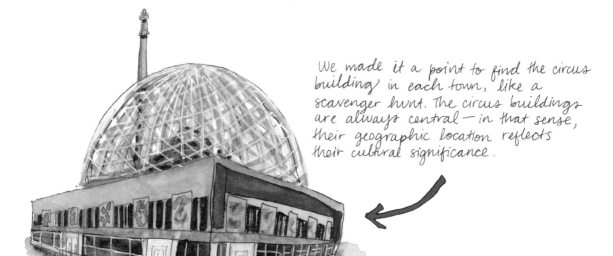

We made it a point to find the circus building in each town, like a scavenger hunt. The circus buildings are always central — in that sense, their geographic location reflects their cultural significance.

We reached the Yekaterinburg circus building by walking along the Iset River, which curves through the city. The river had lovely pedestrian walkways running along its banks.

WE ENCOUNTERED A NEW SHOP GENRE IN YEKATERINBURG: SERVE-YOURSELF, SELL-BY-WEIGHT CANDY SHOPS. THERE SEEMED TO BE ONE EVERY FEW STREETS, APPEARING WITH THE SAME FREQUENCY AS HAIR SALONS & CURRENCY EXCHANGE OFFICES. PEOPLE WALKED OUT CONSTANTLY WITH LITTLE BAGS OF WRAPPED CANDIES OR BOXES OF CHOCOLATE. WE DECIDED WE _HAD_ TO GO IN ONE, & AFTER HALF AN HOUR OF WALKING AROUND THE HUNDREDS OF BINS, WE CHOSE SOME HARD CANDIES TO TAKE WITH US ON THE TRAIN.

WE MADE OUR WAY BACK TO THE TRAIN STATION TO CATCH OUR 2:18 PM NIZHNY NOVGOROD-BOUND TRAIN.

march 24, 12:30 PM

WE ARRIVED AT THE STATION EARLY (AS USUAL). WE WAITED & KEPT AN EYE ON THE BIG TIMETABLE DISPLAYING DEPARTURE & ARRIVAL TIMES, MAKING SURE TO CONVERT MOSCOW TIME (SHOWN ON THE TIMETABLE) TO OUR LOCAL TIME (WHAT WE SAW ON OUR WATCHES & PHONES).

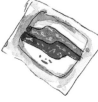

What a delightful surprise! Our **provodnitsa** (train car attendant) came around to hand each passenger a little bag that I came to think of as a "train survival kit." It contained: a wipe to disinfect hands, a wipe to shine shoes, a plastic shoe horn, a toothbrush with very stiff bristles, a miniature tube of toothpaste, & a curved plastic pick that we didn't quite know the use for. We tried the pick on our teeth first but it was way too big, so then we thought it might be for our fingernails. Its true purpose remains a mystery.

WE SETTLED INTO OUR KUPÉ LIKE OLD PROS.
I LOVED HAVING A GRASP ON EVERYTHING,
KNOWING THE PROTOCOL WITH THE PROVODNITSAS,
THE LOCATION OF THE HOT WATER DISPENSER, &
THE POLITE WAY TO ACT IN A SHARED KUPÉ —
BUT PART OF ME MOURNED LOSING THE JITTERY
NEWNESS OF IT ALL. WE WERE BUZZING WHEN
WE BOARDED THE TRAIN IN BEIJING, BUT BY
THIS POINT IN OUR JOURNEY, THOUGH WE WERE
STILL EXCITED, WE WERE TIRED, TOO. I OFTEN
FEEL THAT THE LONGER I TRAVEL, THE DULLER
MY SENSES GET — I THINK IT'S A SORT OF SENSORY
OVERLOAD, DEPLETED ENDORPHINS. I KNOW IT'S A
NATURAL PART OF TRAVEL; WE ARE HUMANS! WE
GET TIRED! BUT SOMETIMES I LOOK BACK ON
CERTAIN DAYS OR EXPERIENCES & WISH I'D BEEN
MORE ALERT. AS OUR TRIP WAS WINDING DOWN,
OUR BODIES & BRAINS WERE TOO. WE USED OUR
TIME ON THE TRAIN TO REST.

LOOKING OUT THE TRAIN WINDOW WAS A WONDERFUL WAY TO REST MY MIND & REGAIN ENERGY. FOR ME, BEING ON THE RAILS WAS A KIND OF NEBULOUS THREAD RUNNING BETWEEN TWO ANCHORED PLACES, A TIME I COULD SPEND IMAGINING WHAT LAY AHEAD AT THE NEXT STOP AS WELL AS RUMINATING ABOUT THE PREVIOUS ONE. THE TRAVEL TIME WAS A PALATE CLEANSER, A NOWHERE LAND.

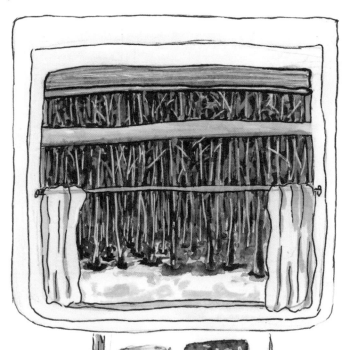

Outside the window, I saw not only white birch trees but also orange-barked trees, a flash of color that stood out starkly against the snowy landscape.

NIZHNY NOVGOROD

march 25, 8:30 AM

SOME 20 HOURS AFTER LEAVING YEKATERINBURG, WE ARRIVED IN NIZHNY NOVGOROD, OUR LAST STOP BEFORE MOSCOW. WE HAD MOVED THROUGH TIME ZONES TOO, & NIZHNY TIME WAS 2 HOURS BEHIND YEKATERINBURG TIME— WE WERE ALWAYS CALCULATING THE TIME DIFFERENCES! THE STATION WAS MODERN, WHICH WAS A BIT OF A LETDOWN AFTER ALL THE WHIMSICAL, BRIGHTLY COLORED TRAIN STATIONS IN SIBERIAN CITIES. THE INTERIOR OF THE STATION, HOWEVER, HAD AN ENORMOUS SOVIET-ERA MOSAIC THAT GREETED US AS WE WALKED FROM THE TRAIN PLATFORM & INTO THE STATION'S MAIN HALL.

Р/Д

ЖЕЛЕЗНОДОРОЖНЫЙ ВОКЗАЛ

Railway station

THIS MASSIVE MOSAIC FROM THE 1960s IS IN THE SOCIALIST REALISM STYLE, THE OFFICIAL ART STYLE IN THE SOVIET UNION FROM THE 1930s TO THE 1980s. SOCIALIST REALISM IS "REALISTIC" IN THE SENSE THAT IT CENTERS THE WORKING CLASS & EVERYDAY LIFE, THOUGH IT'S OFTEN QUITE STYLIZED IN FORM. IDEALIZED LABORERS — HEALTHY, BROAD-SHOULDERED, STRONG — ARE EXALTED & GLORIFIED.

THE CHARACTERS & SCENES IN THIS MOSAIC ARE CLASSIC. IT FEATURES A FARMER WOMAN IN A HEADSCARF HOLDING WHEAT, A TRANSIT AUTHORITY, A SOLDIER, & VARIOUS OTHER PROFESSIONS. BEHIND THESE FIGURES ARE DEPICTIONS OF BOTH INDUSTRIAL & AGRICULTURAL UTOPIA — WITH LENIN PRESIDING OVER IT ALL. THE MOSAIC LOOMS LARGE & RELATES A POINTED POLITICAL MESSAGE TO ALL PASSERSBY: WORKING IS A NOBLE ENDEAVOR, & A DAY'S WORK IS PART OF A GREATER NATIONAL GOOD & WORTHY OF MONUMENTAL REPRESENTATION.

THE CHURCH of THE NATIVITY

march 25, afternoon
WE SET OUT TO EXPLORE THE CITY.
FIRST STOP: the Church of the Nativity.

I couldn't get enough of onion top churches! The church of the Nativity in Nizhny Novgorod did not disappoint. The church was not listed as one of the city's most important ones, but visually, it was my favorite.

BUILT AT THE END OF THE 17TH CENTURY

We went inside the Nativity church & were greeted by a huge gilded altar & beautiful framed icons. Near the altar, a woman stooped to kiss the glass coverings of one icon after another, crossing herself each time. A man waited patiently behind her for his turn at devotion, then followed suit.

THE CHKALOV STAIRS

SOME 800 STEPS, THIS HUGE FLIGHT OF STAIRS CONNECTS MININ & POZHARSKY SQUARES & THE EMBANKMENTS OF THE LOWER & UPPER VOLGA RIVERS. THE STAIRS BEGIN AT THE LOWER BANKS OF THE RIVER & LEAD UP TO THE KREMLIN, WHICH PERCHES ON THE HILL ABOVE. HELVIO STARTED ASCENDING THEM BEFORE ME, & AFTER LESS THAN A MINUTE HE LOOKED LIKE A SMALL DOT, THOUGH HE DIDN'T SEEM TO HAVE MADE MUCH PROGRESS TOWARD THE TOP.

IN RUSSIAN, *KREMLIN* MEANS "FORTRESS"
OR "CITADEL." THE TERM *"THE KREMLIN"*
(CAPITALIZED & WITH NO CITY NAME ATTACHED)
REFERS SPECIFICALLY TO MOSCOW'S
GOVERNMENT SEAT, AKIN TO *"THE WHITE
HOUSE"* IN THE UNITED STATES. BUT MANY
CITIES IN RUSSIA HAVE *KREMLINS*, OR
FORTRESSES, & NIZHNY NOVGOROD'S KREMLIN,
BUILT IN THE EARLY 1500s, IS PARTICULARLY
LOVELY, PROVIDING IMPRESSIVE HILLTOP VIEWS
OVER THE MIGHTY VOLGA & OKA RIVERS AS THEY
FLOW INTO ONE. IT IS FREE TO ENTER THE GROUNDS,
WHICH INCLUDE A NUMBER OF GOVERNMENT
BUILDINGS, 2 MUSEUMS, & A CHURCH.

THE GATE
TO THE **KREMLIN**

ГОСПОДИНЪ ОФОРМИТЕЛЬ

WE STUMBLED UPON THE *STRANGEST* STREET SCENE NEAR THE NIZHNY KREMLIN:
A 12-FOOT-HIGH PINK ELEPHANT, A 10-FOOT-LONG BLUE CARRIAGE, & A MENAGERIE
OF OTHER ANIMAL FIGURINES LINED UP ALONG THE SIDEWALK IN FRONT OF A
SMALL SHOP IN A 2-STORY BRICK BUILDING. THE SHOP, CALLED *GOSPODIN OFORMITEL*,
OR *"MISTER DESIGNER,"* WAS CLOSED & WE WERE LEFT TO WONDER WHAT THIS
PLACE COULD POSSIBLY BE. WE'RE STILL NOT EXACTLY SURE: LATER SLEUTHING REVEALED
THERE IS A SOVIET ART HOUSE HORROR MOVIE TITLED "GOSPODIN OFORMITEL" (1987),
BUT IT DOES NOT INVOLVE LARGE EERIE ANIMAL FIGURES, AS FAR AS I COULD TELL.
THE 12-FOOT PINK ELEPHANT REMAINS A DREAMLIKE MYSTERY IN MY MEMORY!

ANOTHER INTRIGUING SIGHT: A VAN PARKED ON THE STREET DOUBLING AS A BUTCHER SHOP. THE OWNER SOLD MEAT THROUGH ITS SLIDING DOOR, WHICH HAD BEEN INGENIOUSLY CONVERTED TO MIMIC A SHOP WINDOW AT THE MARKET.

Between the onion top cathedral, large pink elephant, & van meat-seller, Nizhny Novgorod was full of wonders large & small.

LEAVING NIZHNY NOVGOROD WAS BITTERSWEET. WE WERE EXCITED TO SEE MOSCOW, WHICH LOOMED LARGE WITH MYTHIC SIGNIFICANCE. BUT REACHING MOSCOW ALSO MARKED THE END OF OUR TRIP. WE WEREN'T READY FOR IT TO BE OVER – YOU'D THINK WE'D BE SICK OF THE TRAIN BY THEN, BUT WE WEREN'T. WE LOVED THE EXCITEMENT OF EACH CITY, PUNCTUATED BY THE LULLABY OF THE TRAIN RIDE IN BETWEEN. WE WOULD HAVE CONTINUED RIDING THE TRAIN TO THE ENDS OF THE EARTH IF WE COULD.

March 27, 10:50 AM

WE TOOK A HIGH-SPEED COMMUTER TRAIN FROM NIZHNY NOVGOROD TO MOSCOW. AFTER ALL THE SLEEPER TRAINS WE'D BEEN ON, IT WAS JARRING TO ENTER A TRAIN CAR FULL OF FOLKS IN BUSINESS CASUAL ATTIRE INSTEAD OF PAJAMAS & SLIPPERS, WHO CARRIED BRIEFCASES INSTEAD OF SUITCASES. THERE WAS EVEN WI-FI ON BOARD! ON THIS LEG OF THE JOURNEY, MOST PEOPLE STARED INTO THEIR PHONES INSTEAD OF OUT THE WINDOW.

WE LEFT THE RAILWAY STATION &
HEADED TO THE KURSKAYA METRO
STATION NEXT DOOR. WE WERE GREETED
BY IMPOSSIBLY HIGH CEILINGS, GILDED
RELIEF PATTERNS, GIANT NEOCLASSICAL
COLUMNS, & A TRIO OF ENORMOUS
CHANDELIERS WITH 5-POINTED RED
STARS OVER OUR HEADS.

SURREAL & OPULENT, THE STATION WAS
A FITTING FIRST GLIMPSE OF MOSCOW,
SURPASSING OUR LARGER-THAN-LIFE
EXPECTATIONS FOR THE CAPITAL CITY.

THE STATION FELT MORE LIKE A PALACE
THAN A TRANSPORT HUB. I IMMEDIATELY
SET OUT VISUALLY COLLECTING 5-POINTED-
STAR & HAMMER-&-SICKLE COMMUNIST
IMAGERY INCORPORATED INTO THE
ELABORATE DECOR.

WE STAYED WITH A LOCAL COUPLE IN A PRIVATE ROOM IN THEIR APARTMENT. THE APARTMENT WAS SMALL BUT LOVELY: A MODEST KITCHEN, A TEENY BATHROOM, OUR ROOM (WHICH OUR SOFA BED CONSUMED WHEN WE PULLED IT OUT EACH NIGHT), & THE COUPLE'S BEDROOM NEXT TO OURS, WHICH WE NEVER SAW. BREAKFAST WAS INCLUDED WITH THE ROOM, PREPARED & ELEGANTLY SET OUT FOR US EACH MORNING BY OUR HOSTESS, WHO WAS A TALENTED COOK & OFFERED RUSSIAN COOKING CLASSES ON THE SIDE.

WE ARRIVED AT THE APARTMENT AROUND 4 PM. AFTER GETTING SETTLED, WE VENTURED OUT TO EXPLORE THE NEIGHBORHOOD. THE APARTMENT WAS NEAR BELORUSSKAYA METRO STATION, IN THE BEGOVOY DISTRICT, WHICH IS DISTINCTLY NONTOURISTIC — LIKE MOST OF MOSCOW, IT'S A MIX OF OFFICE & RESIDENTIAL BUILDINGS. WE HAD A QUIET EVENING, EATING DINNER AT A NEARBY TRADITIONAL RUSSIAN RESTAURANT RECOMMENDED BY OUR HOST & BOOKING A WALKING TOUR OF THE CITY CENTER FOR THE FOLLOWING MORNING.

March 28, 9 AM

WELL RESTED, WE SET OUT AFTER BREAKFAST, TAKING THE METRO TO MEET OUR TOUR GROUP. THE LAST STOP OF THE TOUR — & THE MOST EXCITING PART OF IT — WAS RED SQUARE, FAR & AWAY _THE_ CENTER OF TOURISM IN MOSCOW, & IN MY OPINION, THE SINGLE TOURISM HUB IN THE WHOLE CITY.

MOSCOW

STATE MUSEUM

KAZAN CATHEDRAL

RED SQARE

GUM DEPARTMENT STORE

LENIN'S MAUSOLEUM

KREMLIN WALLS + TOWERS

THE KREMLIN GROUNDS

SAINT BASIL'S CATHEDRAL

MOSKVA RIVER

Visiting Red Square can easily take a full day or more, depending on how many museums & churches you go into.

SAINT BASIL'S CATHEDRAL

FAMILIARLY REFERRED TO AS "SAINT BASIL'S," THIS ICONIC RUSSIAN ORTHODOX CHURCH'S OFFICIAL NAME IS INTERCESSION CHURCH. THE NICKNAME COMES FROM A SINGLE CHAPEL THAT WAS ERECTED OVER THE GRAVE OF SAINT BASIL (_VASILIY_ IN RUSSIAN). IN 1552, IVAN THE TERRIBLE COMMISSIONED THE CHURCH TO COMMEMORATE HIS VICTORY OVER THE TATAR STRONGHOLD IN KAZAN. THE BUILDING WAS ADDED TO OVER THE YEARS, & THE RAINBOW OF COLORS ON THE ONION DOMES THAT ARE SO FAMOUS TODAY WERE LIKELY ADDED DURING AN 18TH CENTURY RESTORATION. (BEFORE THAT, THE DOMES WERE GREEN.)

TODAY, SAINT BASIL'S IS A SYMBOL OF RUSSIA, ITS FOLKLORIC PATTERNS & WHIMSICAL SHAPES BURNING AN INDELIBLE IMAGE OF THE COUNTRY'S CULTURE INTO THE WORLD'S COLLECTIVE CONSCIOUSNESS.

GUM

GUM (PRONOUNCED "*goom*"), MOSCOW'S PREMIER DEPARTMENT STORE, IS TO MOSCOW AS BERGDORF GOODMAN IS TO NEW YORK CITY, OR AS HARROD'S IS TO LONDON. ORNATE & OPULENT, WITH A 780-FOOT-LONG STOREFRONT FACING THE NORTHEAST SIDE OF RED SQUARE, GUM LOOKS MORE LIKE A PALACE THAN A SHOPPING CENTER COMPRISED OF 150 SHOPS. THIS ARCHITECTURAL GRANDEUR GOES HAND IN HAND WITH THE MARXIST-LENINIST PHILOSOPHIES THAT EXALTED THE WORKADAY.

DESIGNED BY A.N. POMERANTSEV & BUILT IN 1889-93, GUM WAS CALLED _GOSUDÁRSTVENNYY UNIVERSÁL'NYY MAGAZIN_, OR STATE DEPARTMENT STORE, DURING THE SOVIET UNION ERA (1922-1991). WHEN THE BUSINESS WAS PRIVATIZED IN 2005, IT WAS STRATEGICALLY RENAMED _MAIN_ DEPARTMENT STORE — THE RUSSIAN WORD FOR "MAIN" IS _GLÁVNYY_, SO GUM REMAINED GUM DESPITE THE NAME CHANGE.

LIGHT FLOWS THROUGH GUM'S DOMED SKYLIGHT ROOF — WHICH CONSISTS OF 20,000 PANES OF GLASS — & IMBUES THE STONE INTERIOR WITH A WARM GLOW. THE ROOF WAS CONSIDERED A REMARKABLE FEAT OF ENGINEERING WHEN IT WAS CONSTRUCTED AT THE END OF THE 19TH CENTURY & IT'S STOOD THE TEST OF TIME: IT'S STILL IMPRESSIVE TO SEE TODAY!

We walked around GUM's multiple levels. We couldn't afford to shop at fancy shops like Gucci or Prada, but we _could_ afford ice creams & a shoeshine.

 ← CURRANT

PISTACHIO ↘

GUM'S ICE CREAM IS LEGENDARY! IT'S BEEN SERVED HERE SINCE 1954 & IS KNOWN FOR USING ONLY NATURAL INGREDIENTS.

EVEN THE SHOESHINE KIOSK WAS STEEPED IN GRANDEUR.

LIKE A KING ON A THRONE, HELVIO SAT UPON A RAISED CHAIR WITHIN A NICHE, WITH THE SHOESHINER PERCHED ON A STOOL AT HIS FEET. HELVIO, SO UNASSUMING BY NATURE, SEEMED A LITTLE EMBARRASSED TO BE SITTING SO PROMINENTLY DISPLAYED FOR ALL PASSERSBY, BUT WATCHING HIM GET HIS SHOES SHINED — MAYBE "CLEANED" IS A BETTER TERM — WAS LOTS OF FUN FOR ME. THE SHOESHINER HAD HIS WORK CUT OUT FOR HIM: THOSE BOOTS HAD BEEN THROUGH SIBERIAN SNOW, ACROSS THE MONGOLIAN STEPPE, & ON & OFF COUNTLESS TRAINS IN THE WEEKS PRIOR. THEY LOOKED A BIT THE WORSE FOR WEAR & WERE VASTLY IMPROVED BY THE SHOESHINER'S SKILLFUL WORK.

Чистка обуви

STOLOVAYA 57

OUR WALKING TOUR GUIDE RECOMMENDED WE TRY STOLOVAYA 57, LOCATED ON THE TOP FLOOR OF GUM, FOR LUNCH. THE PRICES WERE FINE & THE FOOD GOOD TOO, BUT THE SOVIET-NOSTALGIA DECOR MADE ME FEEL LIKE I WAS IN A MOVIE SET VERSION OF A STOLOVAYA.

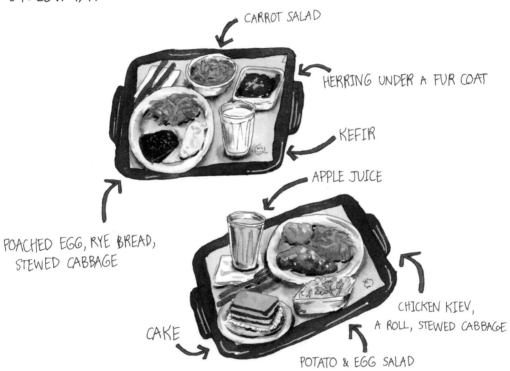

CARROT SALAD

HERRING UNDER A FUR COAT

KEFIR

APPLE JUICE

POACHED EGG, RYE BREAD, STEWED CABBAGE

CHICKEN KIEV, A ROLL, STEWED CABBAGE

CAKE

POTATO & EGG SALAD

PLUS, IT SEEMED TO BE MOSTLY FOREIGN TOURISTS LIKE US DINING THERE — WHICH WAS FINE, EXCEPT THAT ONE OF MY FAVORITE THINGS ABOUT EATING AT MORE LOCALLY FREQUENTED EATERIES WAS CHECKING OUT WHAT RUSSIANS WERE EATING & LOADING UP MY OWN TRAY WITH THE SAME! I WILL SAY, THOUGH, STOLOVAYA 57 WAS ONE OF THE MOST BUDGET-FRIENDLY PLACES TO EAT IN THE HIGHLY TOURISTIC &, CORRESPONDINGLY, VERY EXPENSIVE RED SQUARE VICINITY.

MOSCOW METRO TOUR

FOR LESS THAN **$1**, YOU CAN TRAVEL IN THIS UNDERGROUND TREASURE FOR AS LONG AS YOU WANT. IT'S PRACTICALLY FREE! WE VISITED ON A PARTICULARLY COLD & WINDY DAY, SO WE ENJOYED THE ADDED BENEFIT OF STAYING WARM.

THE METRO IS SO STUNNING THAT IT IS, IN FACT, A TOURIST DESTINATION IN ITS OWN RIGHT. IT IS SO IMPROBABLY BEAUTIFUL THAT VISITORS SHOULD LOG IT AS A TRIP TO A GREAT MUSEUM AS OPPOSED TO A MERE MEANS OF TRANSPORTATION. IT'S SO VAST (ITS 194 STATIONS COVER 202 MILES) THAT EVEN THOUGH WE SPENT A FULL DAY UNDERGROUND WE COULDN'T VISIT ANYWHERE NEAR ALL THE STATIONS WE WANTED TO.

STALIN INITIATED THE CONSTRUCTION OF THE MOSCOW METRO IN THE EARLY 1930s, & THE FIRST LINE OPENED IN 1935. PROGRESSIVELY MORE METRO STOPS & LINES WERE CONSTRUCTED AS THE YEARS WENT ON — & THAT EXPANSION CONTINUES TODAY, AS THE METRO'S GROWTH MATCHES THE CITY'S.

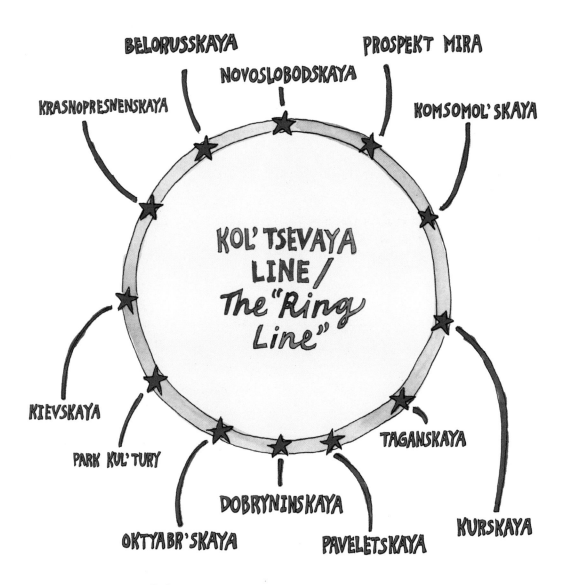

BELORUSSKAYA

PROSPEKT MIRA

NOVOSLOBODSKAYA

KRASNOPRESNENSKAYA

KOMSOMOL'SKAYA

KOL'TSEVAYA
LINE/
The "Ring
Line"

KIEVSKAYA

TAGANSKAYA

PARK KUL'TURY

DOBRYNINSKAYA

KURSKAYA

OKTYABR'SKAYA

PAVELETSKAYA

THE "RING LINE" SITS ON A CIRCULAR TRACK THAT TRAVELS AROUND THE CITY CENTER. BUILT IN THE 1950s, IT HAS SOME OF THE MOST FAMOUSLY ORNATE STATIONS, LIKE KOMSOMOL'SKAYA. THIS LINE MAKES FOR A NO-BRAINER ITINERARY: JUST HOP ON THE METRO & KEEP GOING TIL YOU GET BACK WHERE YOU STARTED!

225

ЛЕНИН

Komsomol'skaya Station

ceiling mosaic
in Belorusskaya station

I TRIED TO LOG ALL THE 5-POINTED STARS & HAMMERS & SICKLES I SAW, BUT I QUICKLY LOST COUNT—THERE WERE SO MANY! MY FAVORITES WERE THOSE I CAME UPON IN UTILITARIAN PLACES: ON HEATING GRATES, FOR INSTANCE, OR INCORPORATED INTO BARELY PERCEPTIBLE RAISED MEDALLIONS THAT ALL BUT BLENDED INTO THE WALL.

NOVOSLOBODSKAYA STATION

THE 32 ARCHED STAINED GLASS WINDOWS IN NOVOSLOBODSKAYA STATION ARE INCREDIBLE. *NOTABLE*: THE LARGE ARCHED MOSAIC AT ONE END, "*PEACE IN THE WHOLE WORLD*," LIKE SO MANY SOVIET-ERA DEPICTIONS OF WOMEN, SHOWS A FEMALE FARMER SURROUNDED BY GOLDEN WHEAT, A SYMBOL OF AGRICULTURE, & HOLDING A BABY ALOFT. THE DOVES ABOVE THE WOMAN'S HEAD ARE A RECENT ADDITION: THEY REPLACED THE ORIGINAL PORTRAIT OF STALIN.

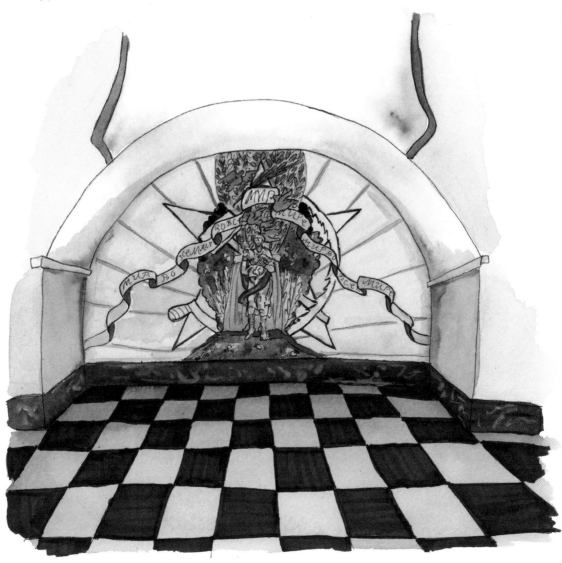

stained glass panels in
Art Nouveau style. They are
lit from within, which
makes them luminous & bright.

A commuter in a
fabulous fur coat,
waiting next to us
on the platform.

For breakfast each morning, I requested <u>kasha</u>, Russian buckwheat porridge. It was cooked perfectly in a traditional single-serving clay pot, with milk, butter, & a sprinkling of seeds on top. Dobroye utro! (Good morning!)

WE SPENT OUR FINAL DAY IN MOSCOW EXPLORING GORKY PARK.
IT'S FAMOUS FOR ITS NATURAL BEAUTY &, IN THE SUMMER, FULL OF
VISITORS EXERCISING, LOUNGING, & SOCIALIZING. BUT IN SPRING —
RUSSIANS' LEAST FAVORITE TIME OF YEAR, AS IT'S STILL COLD
BUT THE SNOW MELTS, LEAVING EVERYTHING MUDDY — THE PARK
WAS DESERTED.

I DIDN'T MIND THE FEELING OF SOLITUDE AS WE TRAVERSED THE
EXTENSIVE GROUNDS. AND IN FACT, THE EMPTINESS ENDED UP
LENDING ITSELF TO THE MOOD OF THE SCULPTURE GARDEN. THE
MUZEON PARK OF ARTS WAS MY ABSOLUTE FAVORITE: IT HOUSES A
NUMBER OF SOVIET-ERA-COMMISSIONED SCULPTURES THAT WERE
REMOVED FROM PUBLIC PLACES AFTER THE SOVIET UNION COLLAPSED
IN 1991. FOR THIS REASON, THE SCULPTURE DISPLAY AREA IS ALSO
CALLED THE "PARK OF FALLEN MONUMENTS."

I WAS MOVED AS I WALKED AMONG THESE LONELY SCULPTURES,
BANISHED FROM THEIR HOMES, NOW OUT OF CONTEXT. THERE
WAS SOMETHING EERIE ABOUT THEM. WE WALKED AMONG
THE FALLEN MONUMENTS IN SILENCE.

AND JUST LIKE THAT: OUR TRIP WAS OVER. TIME FELT LIKE AN ACCORDION, EXPANDING (HOW DID WE SEE, HEAR, FEEL, & TASTE SO MUCH IN SUCH A SHORT PERIOD OF TIME?) & CONTRACTING (HOW COULD IT BE OVER WHEN WE'D BARELY BEGUN?).

WHEN WE PLANNED OUR JOURNEY ON THE TRANS-SIBERIAN RAILWAY, WE BILLED IT AS A ONCE-IN-A-LIFETIME TRIP. IT SEEMED LIKE SOMETHING TO EXPERIENCE, YES, BUT ALSO TO COMPLETE. THE REALITY WAS MUCH DIFFERENT. WE IMMEDIATELY BEGAN DISCUSSING THE POSSIBILITY OF TAKING THE RAILWAY AGAIN, BUT THIS TIME STARTING IN MOSCOW & ENDING IN VLADIVOSTOK.

PERHAPS THIS GETS AT THE ROOT OF WHY A TRIP ON THE TRANS-SIBERIAN CANNOT BE COMPLETED, OR TIED IN A NEAT BOW, OR CHECKED OFF A LIST. IT'S NOT SINGULAR. THE PERMUTATIONS ARE ENDLESS & CHANGE DEPENDING ON WHEN YOU TRAVEL, WHICH OF THE 3 ROUTES YOU TAKE, THE TRAINS YOU CATCH, THE CLASS YOU SELECT, WHO YOUR FELLOW PASSENGERS ARE, THE CITIES YOU STOP IN, & HOW LONG YOU STAY. UPON COMPLETING OUR JOURNEY FROM BEIJING TO MOSCOW, IT CLICKED FOR ME: ONE TAKES _A_ TRANS-SIBERIAN RAILWAY, NOT _THE_ TRANS-SIBERIAN RAILWAY. MY CURIOSITY ABOUT THE TRIP IN ALL ITS VARIATIONS INTENSIFIED INSTEAD OF DIMINISHING.

WE THOUGHT A JOURNEY ON THE TRANS-SIBERIAN WAS AN ITCH THAT WE, AS AVID TRAVELERS, COULD SCRATCH. IT WASN'T. IF THE TRANS-SIBERIAN IS AN ITCH, IT ITCHES US STILL — PERHAPS MORE NOW THAN IT DID BEFORE WE BOARDED THE TRAIN IN BEIJING. WE HOPE TO RETURN TO THE RAILS SOON.

ACKNOWLEDGMENTS

HELVIO – because the only thing I like as much as traveling with you is being at home with you.

ELIZABETH VISCOTT SULLIVAN – for clarity of vision & for pushing me to craft a narrative from bits & pieces — for emboldening me to write more — & for an impeccable instinct for knowing when to expand & when to whittle down. The shape of this book is because of you.

LIZ NEALON – for seeing me & believing in my work from the jump, a calming presence & source of sage advice in all things.

CHARLOTTE SHEEDY – for leading me to Liz.

MAGGIE – always my first call.

MAMA, PAPA, & SAM – for doing me (too many) favors — always, but especially in 2016 & 2017 during my nomadic years.

Border Crossings

HarperCollins books may be purchased for educational, business, or sales promotional use. For information, please e-mail the Special Markets Department at SPsales@harpercollins.com.

First published in 2022 by
Harper Design
An Imprint of HarperCollins Publishers
195 Broadway
New York, NY 10007
Tel: (212) 207-7000
Fax: (855) 746-6023

harperdesign@harpercollins.com
www.hc.com

Distributed throughout the world by
HarperCollins Publishers
195 Broadway
New York, NY 10007

ISBN 978-0-06-308036-2
Library of Congress Control Number: 2021033018

Book & cover design by Emma Fick

Printed in Malaysia

First Printing, 2022

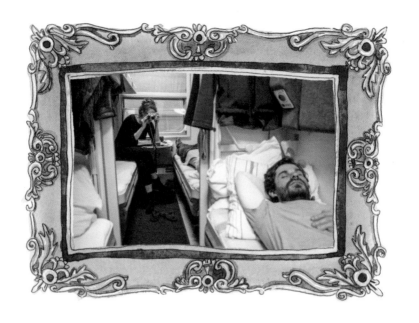

EMMA FICK IS AN ARTIST & ILLUSTRATOR. AFTER COMPLETING HER DEGREE IN ENGLISH LITERATURE & ART HISTORY IN 2013, SHE TAUGHT ENGLISH IN SERBIA ON A FULBRIGHT SCHOLARSHIP & BEGAN TO CHRONICLE SERBIAN CULTURE IN A SERIES OF WATERCOLOR ILLUSTRATIONS SHE CALLED "SNIPPETS." WITH A GRANT FROM THE US EMBASSY, EMMA RETURNED TO SERBIA TO PURSUE PAINTING FULL-TIME. AFTER PUBLISHING HER FIRST BOOK OF ILLUSTRATIONS, _SNIPPETS OF SERBIA_, IN 2015, SHE RETURNED HOME TO LOUISIANA & BEGAN _SNIPPETS OF NEW ORLEANS_, WHICH WAS PUBLISHED IN 2017. SHE HOPES TO CONTINUE TRAVELING FAR & WIDE, ILLUSTRATING HER WAY ACROSS THE WORLD. SHE LIVES IN NEW ORLEANS.